DATE DUE FOR RETURN		
XXXXXX 89		

REVOLUTION
AND THE
RULE OF LAW

EDWARD KENT

teaches Philosophy of Law
at Brooklyn College, City University of New York.

A member of the Church-State Committee
of the American Civil Liberties Union,
he is the editor of
Law and Philosophy: Readings in Legal Philosophy.

REVOLUTION AND THE RULE OF LAW

Edited by
Edward Kent

Prentice-Hall, Inc. A SPECTRUM BOOK *Englewood Cliffs, N.J.*

PRENTICE-HALL INTERNATIONAL, INC. (*London*)
PRENTICE-HALL OF AUSTRALIA, PTY. LTD. (*Sydney*)
PRENTICE-HALL OF CANADA, LTD. (*Toronto*)
PRENTICE-HALL OF INDIA PRIVATE LIMITED (*New Delhi*)
PRENTICE-HALL OF JAPAN, INC. (*Tokyo*)

Contents

viii

About the Contributors

PHILIP BERRIGAN, S.S.J., and his brother Daniel Berrigan, S.J., are well-known activists in the Catholic peace movement who have both been imprisoned for acts of resistance.

GIDON GOTTLIEB was educated at Trinity College, Cambridge, and received his doctorate at Harvard Law School. He is the author of *The Logic of Choice: An Investigation of the Concepts of Rule and Rationality* (1968) and has served as consultant to the United Nations and to President Johnson's Commission on Human Rights Year.

VIRGINIA HELD, Professor of Philosophy at Hunter College, City University of New York, has contributed numerous articles to political journals and is the author of *The Public Interest and Individual Interests* (1970).

MARTIN LUTHER KING, JR., civil rights leader, Nobel Prize winner, needs no formal introduction. "Letter from Birmingham City Jail" is perhaps his most eloquent defense of the tactics of nonviolent civil disobedience as an instrument of social reform.

HERBERT MARCUSE is Professor of Philosophy at the University of California, San Diego. He has published extensively in English and German, and his books include *Reason and Revolution* (1941), *Eros and Civilization* (1955), *Soviet Marxism* (1958), and *One Dimensional Man* (1964).

ALFRED G. MEYER is Professor of Political Science at the University of Michigan. Among his publications are *The Soviet Political System* (1966) and *Marxism: The Unity of Theory and Practice* (1970).

JOHN RAWLS is Professor of Philosophy at Harvard University and author of major essays in political theory.

BOBBY SEALE, co-founder with Huey P. Newton of the Black Panther Party, at this writing faces charges of alleged conspiracy on several counts in Chicago.

MICHAEL WALZER, Professor of Government at Harvard University, is the author of *The Revolution of the Saints* (1965) and *Obligations: Essays on Disobedience, War, and Citizenship* (1970).

ROBERT PAUL WOLFF is Professor of Philosophy at the University of Massachusetts. He has offered major criticisms of classical liberalism in his books *The Poverty of Liberalism* (1968) and *In Defense of Anarchism* (1970).

EDWARD KENT

Introduction

The essays collected here speak to current felt wrongs in American life, suggest ways to protest them, argue new perspectives upon our political and legal traditions, and claim new justifications for active political dissent. That there is no consensus among these authors is evidence of the diversity of possible perspectives on recent history and the complexities of economic, political, and social structures that challenge those engaged in reform.

Contemporary dissenters face a common dilemma: rule of law is a central democratic ideal and yet illegal forms of protest have accompanied significant reforms in the past and seem necessary to many to accomplish, or at least speed, much-needed contemporary advances. Recent disruptions scarcely begin to match the cost in lives and property of past national crises. The nation was born in revolution. It has seen the near extinction of the American Indian. The New York draft riots of 1863 alone took more than a thousand lives. We have survived a civil war with an enduring heritage of racial violence and sectional enmity. Forms of contemporary protest echo old models: court disruptions by the suffragettes and prohibitionists, Canada as refuge for runaway slaves; arson, bombing, political assassination, illegal strikes against property interests, violence and counterviolence mark the history of our protest movements.

New Problems and Possibilities

Students of political theory have been increasingly impressed by the inadequacies of some of our traditional models of political obligation. Stemming from the simpler worlds of eighteenth-century agriculture and commerce and assuming a tightly knit, largely ho-

1

mogeneous society bound by common interests, the social-contract heritage embedded in our national ideology scarcely accounts for the complex power-realities of modern industrial states rent by racial, ethnic, and economic conflicts. The suffering of currently oppressed groups—the poor, the politically impotent, the racially oppressed, the innocent victims of modern warfare—has touched and torments the conscience of honest men. Our awareness of things that must be changed exceeds our present instruments for necessary reforms. We have discovered new social and economic priorities and possibilities but also face new potential tyrannies and man-made disasters. We are divided as much by miscommunication and the echos of dying ideologies as by the complexities of our pragmatic concerns. In such a context we must expect, if not always welcome, new modes of protest against felt tyrannies.

The first two essays reprinted here mark the end of an era. Shortly before his death, Martin Luther King, Jr. pondered the new methods that might be needed to move a lethargic body politic beyond the relatively inexpensive civil rights that had thus far been granted to the vast and costly programs necessary to eradicate poverty and its lingering effects. John Rawls recently remarked that some form of socialism may be a necessary supplement to his own program of "justice as fairness."

The remainder of these essays explore alternative strategies of protest and reform. Herbert Marcuse, Philip Berrigan, and Bobby Seale speak of several types of revolution. Robert Wolff defends anarchism and analyzes the nature and sources of violence. Gidon Gottlieb proposes a new vision of law based on the arbitration models of labor and international law. Michael Walzer and Virginia Held consider disobedience in the context of new political models. Alfred Meyer studies civil disobedience in Russia and Eastern Europe and discovers surprising similarities in the tactics of protest used in liberal democracies and those employed in authoritarian regimes—with perhaps greater sophistication of manoeuver displayed by citizens in the latter repressive contexts.

Terminological Disputes

Divergent usage of basic terms in the lexicon of protest movements confronts the commentator with an immediate problem in communication. "Revolution," traditionally seen as the overthrow of an established government, has acquired new meanings. Herbert Marcuse suggests that revolution must involve radical changes in social structures to be distinguished from mere *coup* or "palace" revolution. Philip Berrigan scores revolutionary violence and sees nonviolent progress as the mark of true revolution. Bobby Seale employs the new revolutionary rhetoric but calls for the fulfilment of old American ideals: constitutional rights and "life, liberty and the pursuit of happiness for all."

"Civil disobedience" is a similarly ranging concept. At one extreme it is equated with revolution; at the other, it is narrowly restricted to include only apparently illegal acts that will be eventually judicially vindicated. John Rawls represents civil disobedience as a "public, nonviolent, conscientious act contrary to law usually done with the intent to bring about change in the policies or laws of the government . . . where arrest and punishment are expected and accepted without resistance." Rawls is following a developed philosophic tradition that formalizes the practical models of Mohandas Gandhi and Dr. King. This moderate definition has its attractive features and can serve as a standard for some forms of protest. But as a definition it suffers from significant liabilities: its restricting criteria exclude many acts that have traditionally been considered civilly disobedient. The Underground Railroad and other types of dissidence in their formative stages have been necessarily secretive. Violence or the threat of violence have been employed as tactics by many subsequently litanized for their contributions to reform—the abolitionists, the suffragettes, labor organizers, farm-mortgage rebels. The conscientiousness of any act of protest is questioned almost automatically by opponents; one man's conscientious act is another's outrage. Acceptance of arrest and punishment arbitrarily precludes flight from same—slavery or military service.

This moderate definition also tends to redirect attention from the aims of protesters and the consequences of their acts to tactical considerations. Potentially disastrous strikes by public officials, public-service employees, and medical personal would qualify as instances of civil disobedience, while relatively modest forms of protest, such as burning draft files and flight from arrest, would not.

In the face of such disadvantages it seems reasonable to retain the more traditional and loosely-framed standard that simply identifies civil disobedience with some limited reform-goal short of full-scale, violent revolution, whatever the tactics employed. In articulating his selective aims, the disobedient distinguishes himself from the revolutionary or mindless rioter. Virginia Held further examines subtypes of civil disobedience within this general frame.

The Justification Impasse

While recent literature on social protest has frequently attempted to transfer standards of justification common in moral philosophy to the legal-political sphere, sets of binding principles derived from this source have been of little practical assistance either to protesters or courts called upon to judge their acts. I would argue that such formal systems fail because of a fundamental impass that pits the moral assumptions of protesters against the formal obligations of legal officials. The dissenter presumably considers his illegal acts justified or else he would not commit them; judges are bound by oath of office to punish crimes. Each side faces the impasse suggested by Hobbes' all-too-contemporary observation: "[A] man commanded as a soldier to fight against the enemy, though his sovereign have right enough to punish his refusal with death, may nevertheless in many cases refuse without injustice. . . ."

The impasse is not new. It represents an almost endemic conflict between moral and legal systems. Catholic natural-law theorists during the nineteenth century all but bankrupted the doctrine in factional disputes over private property rights, the application of just-war criteria, etc. Human-rights doctrines generally suffer from a gap between high-level principle and concrete prescription. Locke's trilogy of inalienable rights (life, liberty, and property) carried with it no means for weighting these interests. Until most recently, dominant property interests have tended to win over the rights of life and liberty in Anglo-American practice. The "equal-liberty" criterion for founding rights proposed by Rousseau, developed by Kant, and reconceived by Professor Rawls has not resolved in practice disputes, for instance, between those who demand "freedom now" and those who defend gradual reform. Such principles are ambiguous or irrelevant if applied to contemporary conflicts—war-resistance, allocation of national resources, special-group needs. Such formulae may identify instances of extreme inequity but scarcely touch the surface of issues dividing competing interests.

Political Obligation Reviewed

What is wrong with our traditional models of political obligation? John Locke's version of the social contract was severely criticized by John Stuart Mill, who complained that majority rule was all too readily convertible into "tyranny of the majority," the tendency of ascendant majorities to ride rough-shod over minority interests. As a critic in turn of Mill, Robert Wolff has developed an engaging "defense of anarchism" (title of one of his recent books), which argues the universalization of consent as the only justifiable basis of political obligation. Scrutiny of the two positions reveals flaws in each.

Locke had proposed that individuals living in a state of nature would be bound by reason to found through mutual contract a superior and impartial judicial authority. An independant party was necessary to adjudicate the occasional conflicts that might arise among even moral individuals. Locke, however, was forced to bolster the simple structure of contract with fictions: that subsequent members of a contracting society would be bound by tacit consent to its legislative directives, that individuals shortchanged by the contract retained only the options of emigration (to America) or active revolution. Some of his subsidiary claims for sovereign authority are simply abhorrent in the face of contemporary events: he commended, for instance, "absolute obedience to the command of every superior officer, and it is justly death to disobey or dispute the most dangerous or unreasonable of them. . . ." Despite Locke's formal claim of inalienable rights against sovereign power, no standard contract today would permit such far-ranging commitment to unforeseen obligations. One party to a normal contract cannot change set terms (legislate) unilaterally. Even Locke recognized that independent judges should settle individual disputes; yet his sovereign authority is a party to his social compact.

Political anarchism does not recognize the need for any society to impose obligations upon its members, with or without their consent. One can make the claim, but it does not resolve the need for arbitrators of cases of hard conflict between interests that are bound to arise in any community. Perhaps the nearest approach in practice to political anarchism, classical liberalism and its *laissez-faire* doctrines of economics, failed because it could guarantee neither minimal standards of justice nor the fiction of consent itself. Tyranny of the majority is just as much a prospect with anarchism as under existing systems of legal rule. Bentham's panopticon remains with us.

Turning from consent-based models of obligation to Thomas Hobbes' *Leviathan,* written out of the chaos of the British revolution in the seventeenth century, we find at least a realistic account of the power-factors at play in modern states. Hobbes' contract formula made no pretense of limitations upon state authority. His contract was made between individuals in a state of war and desperately in need of a common authority to maintain peace. There were no niceties about inalienable rights: subjects' liberties lay "only in those things which in regulating their actions, the sovereign pretermitted . . ."

Adapting Hobbes to present conditions, we would find a citizen with only three options: 1) he could endorse actively an existing government and its policies, 2) he might accept them only passively, and 3) at his own risk he could actively protest. The first two options, concurring actively or *passively,* constitute two forms of political consent. The only true dissent is active protest. This distinction is lost in democracies that permit extensive freedoms of speech—verbal dissent—but is all too readily apparent in authoritarian regimes that punish dissent as a political crime.

A departure from Hobbes' scheme is necessary, of course, to account for contemporary protest short of full-scale revolution. Hobbes' sovereign, supreme and unified, encompassed all legal and political authority. The slightest resistance entailed direct challenge to sovereign rule entire. We now recognize the multiple agencies of modern governments. It is possible to protest a selected law, policy, or official act while still maintaining wider allegiance to the rule of law.

The advantage in approaching political obligation with a Hobbesian sensibility lies in his recognition of the fact that individuals do not bind themselves because they have consented to a form of government, but rather consent because they are obliged by other interests. For Hobbes, "security" was the primary stimulus for social contract. Similarly, Kant, writing in the context of his philosophy of law, did not mince words over the sources of obligation:

> Certainly, a state of nature need not be a condition of injustice . . . it is, however, still a state of society in which justice is absent . . . and in which, when there is controversy concerning rights, no competent judge can be found to render a decision having the force of law. For this reason, everyone may use violent means to compel another to enter into a juridical state of society.

In modern translation, many interests apart from, and overriding, consent form the basis of our political obligations: interests in general social welfare, social justice, progress, conservation of human and natural resources, etc. We may be justly forced by juridical authority to do, or abstain from doing, things we would not otherwise choose. Consent, of course, is ideally a correlate of political obligation, but neither a necessary nor sufficient condition of it. The justifiable nature and extent of political coercion, not the fact of it, is our appropriate normative concern.

Beyond the Social Contract: Social Interests

Underlying the Hobbesian contract and already well-developed in our native pragmatic tradition of American jurisprudence is the notion that interests—individual and social—constitute the cement that holds modern societies together. William James observed: "Since everything which is demanded is by that fact a good, must not the guiding principle for ethical philosophy (since all demands conjointly cannot be satisfied in this poor world) be simply to satisfy at all times as many demands as we can." Dean Roscoe Pound responded with his elaborated theory of social interests. Traditional interests in general security, general morals, and the maintenance of existing institutions must be supplemented by newly conceived interests in conservation, progress, and quality of individual life, Pound argued early in this century. The New Deal saw the energetic implementation of many of his proposals. Pound offered a new perspective on social reality that broke with the older model of individual consent between equal parties to give recognition to the unequal distribution of power among interest groups. His call was for a redress of power-realities, or at least the recognition of inequities hidden by the stance of older doctrines. To quote him at length on the subject of balancing labor and management interests:

> When it comes to weighing or valuing claims or demands with respect to other claims or demands, we must be careful to compare them on the same plane. If we put one as an individual interest and the other as a social interest we may decide the question in advance in our very way of putting it. For example, in the "truck act" cases one may think of the claim of the employer to make contracts freely as an individual interest of substance. In that event, we must weigh it with the claim of the employee not to be coerced by economic pressure into making contracts to take his pay in orders on a company store, thought of as an individual personality. If we think of either in terms of a policy we must think of the other in the same terms. If we think of the employee's claim in terms of a policy of assuring a minimum or standard human life, we must think of the employer's claim in terms of a policy of upholding and enforcing contracts. If one is thought of as a right and the other as a policy, or if the one is thought of as an individual interest and the other a social interest, our way of stating the question may leave nothing to decide.

Articulated claims and demands have changed radically since Pound first published these words in 1921. But his vision of society caught up in an ever-changing web of competing interests has been more than substantiated recently by political scientists' behavioral analyses of the power-realities underlying our formal constitutional structure of rule of law. Not individual consent but constantly shifting and only sometimes countervailing power-groupings determine national policies. The dynamics of domestic policy-formation makes a mockery of consent-theory. The alienated or continually subordinated interest-group cannot be said to have promised anything in the way of consent to a continually shifting balance of power-interests. Even majority rule cannot be justified by consent-theory, although it is sometimes justified by the interests which it serves. Plato himself was obliged to ballast consent with secondary considerations of interest, in his well-known defense of fidelity to law, in the *Crito*: ". . . thrice wrong; first, because in disobeying his parents; secondly, because we are the authors of his education; thirdly, because he has made an agreement with us that he will duly obey our commands; and that he neither obeys them nor convinces us that our commands are unjust . . ."). How much irony here? Justice is still the interest of the stronger.

The virtue of political protest—especially in democracies—is that it can challenge consensually-arrived-at majority-tyranny. As Gidon Gottlieb notes, dissent has proved itself as a powerful form of veto over dominant interests. General security can be undermined by violent acts; encumbent administrations can be driven from office by judicious use of public protest.

It must be stressed in this context that the move from social contract to social-interest theory does not entail the end of political obligation but rather suggests new and vital sources of it. If allegiance by individuals to the state as monolith can no longer be guaranteed, nevertheless, the loyalties of subordinate groups may be sought and won when their interests are allowed expression and satisfied in the wider balance of competing claims and demands. Interest groupings constitute a potential intermediate nexus of obligations between individuals and their society at large. If disenchanted with national policies, potential dissenters still retain links of obligation to their subgroup and, presumably, must play out the game of power politics with its interests in mind. Dominant groups not infrequently counter dissent with repressive measures. Not simply the sense of justice of one's cause but also potential consequences for one's group play a central role in dissenting strategies. An individual may risk his own interests but not those of his group since they are now vested with a value comparable to that of the entire body politic in the older contract-model. The choice of tactics for dissenters may make the difference between vindication and defeat of the particular claim in question. As Martin Luther King, Jr. notes in his "Letter," mature acts of dissent must be preceded by deliberate stages ["1) Collection of the facts to determine whether injustices are alive. 2) Negotiation. 3) Self-purification"] before the final step of protest is undertaken.

The Right to Protest?

What right do individuals have to protest felt wrongs, either as individuals or as representatives of larger groups? In the narrower sense of a legally protected right, it has been pointed out that protest involves an impasse that finds legal officials bound to punish illegal acts. In practice, however, it is obvious that officials variously use their considerable discretionary powers, sometimes to mitigate punishment, sometimes to aggravate it. Protest involves one of our most unsettled areas of contemporary law, and bases of expectation here are slight and controlled by numerous accidental factors. District attorneys may vary the severity of charges involving similar physical acts; some federal jurisdictions routinely punish draft resistance with sentences considerably more severe than others. Manifestly, the potential protester must weigh punishments in determining which tactics most efficiently accomplish his aims. The popular acceptance of his cause, the degree and kind of political support he has won, even the jurisdiction within which he may be tried, can make the greatest difference in determining the consequences he will suffer.

Should we punish political protesters? Many men of good will both in the legal and philosophic communities have sought grounds by which protesters might be absolved from punishment. Although protesters have frequently been excused for minor infractions, no practical scheme has been designed for exonerating serious crimes committed as protest, especially those that threaten human welfare. Short of a full revolutionary stance that denies all legitimacy to the legal system, equal punishment for serious crimes seems a rooted and universal standard of justice.

What rights should protesters retain? The phenomenon of conscientious protest has heightened our consciousness of the inhumane treatment of prisoners that passes for reform in the run-of-the-mill of our penal institutions. What earlier generations of reformers planned to be institutions for the reform of character have turned out to be schools for crime, virtually designed to generate hostility toward society. The examples of the Berrigans and Bobby Seale put to the test long-standing penal practices—mindless censorship and denial of human dignity, for example—when humane treatment of prisoners is perfectly feasible even within a restraining prison environment.

Is our present political system equal to the challenge of active protest? As I indicated at the beginning of this introduction, present disruptions by protesters are a mild echo of earlier incidents in our national history. Protest is not incompatible with rule of law nor so threatening to healthy democratic regimes as to justify the suppression of the fundamental rights they were instituted to protect. There seems to be no legitimate reason for the present national hysteria in some quarters that calls for compounded punishment of protesters (e.g., the notorious conspiracy charge and other omnibus bills more characteristic of totalitarian regimes). Our capacity to guarantee the normal legal rights of protesters is perhaps our best barometer of national political health—or distemper. To abandon traditional rights and legal safeguards developed over the nearly 200 years since our last revolution would be its great betrayal.

MARTIN LUTHER KING, JR.

Letter from Birmingham City Jail

My dear Fellow Clergymen,

While confined here in the Birmingham City Jail, I came across your recent statement calling our present activities "unwise and untimely." Seldom, if ever, do I pause to answer criticism of my work and ideas. If I sought to answer all of the criticisms that cross my desk, my secretaries would be engaged in little else in the course of the day, and I would have no time for constructive work. But since I feel that you are men of genuine goodwill and your criticisms are sincerely set forth, I would like to answer your statement in what I hope will be patient and reasonable terms.

I think I should give the reason for my being in Birmingham, since you have been influenced by the argument of "outsiders coming in." I have the honor of serving as president of the Southern Christian Leadership Conference, an organization operating in every Southern state, with headquarters in Atlanta, Georgia. We have some eighty-five affiliate organizations all across the South— one being the Alabama Christian Movement for Human Rights. Whenever necessary and possible we share staff, educational and financial resources with our affiliates. Several months ago our local affiliate here in Birmingham invited us to be on call to engage in a nonviolent direct action program if such were deemed necessary. We readily consented and when the hour came we lived up to our promises. So I am here, along with several members of my staff, because we were invited here. I am here because I have basic organizational ties here.

Beyond this, I am in Birmingham because injustice is here. Just as the eighth century prophets left their little villages and carried their "thus saith the Lord" far beyond the boundaries of their home towns; and just as the Apostle Paul left his little village of Tarsus and carried the gospel of Jesus Christ to practically every hamlet and city of the Graeco-Roman world, I too am compelled to carry the gospel of freedom beyond my particular home town. Like Paul, I must constantly respond to the Macedonian call for aid.

Moreover, I am cognizant of the interrelatedness of all communities and states. I cannot sit idly by in Atlanta and not be concerned about what happens in Birmingham. Injustice anywhere is a threat to justice everywhere. We are caught in an inescapable network of mutuality, tied in a single garment of destiny. Whatever affects one directly affects all indirectly. Never again can we afford to live with the narrow, provincial "outside agitator" idea. Anyone who lives inside the United States can never be considered an outsider anywhere in this country.

You deplore the demonstrations that are presently taking place in Birmingham. But I am sorry that your statement did not express a similar concern for the conditions that brought the demonstrations into being. I am sure that each of you would want to go beyond the superficial social analyst who looks merely at effects, and does not grapple with underlying causes. I would not hesitate to say that it is unfortunate that so-called demonstrations are taking place in Birmingham at this time, but I would say in more emphatic terms that it is even more unfortunate that the white power structure of this city left the Negro community with no other alternative.

In any nonviolent campaign there are four basic steps: 1) Collection of the facts to determine whether injustices are alive. 2) Negotiation. 3) Self-purification and 4) Direct Action. We have gone through all of these steps in Birmingham. There can be no gainsaying of the fact that racial injustice engulfs this community.

Birmingham is probably the most thoroughly segregated city in the United States. Its ugly record of police brutality is known in every section of this country. Its injust treatment of Negroes in the courts is a notorious reality. There have been more unsolved bombings of Negro homes and churches in Birmingham than any city in this nation. These are the hard, brutal and unbelievable facts. On the basis of these conditions Negro leaders sought to negotiate with the city fathers. But the political leaders consistently refused to engage in good faith negotiation.

Then came the opportunity last September to talk with some of the leaders of the economic community. In these negotiating sessions certain promises were made by the merchants—such as the promise to remove the humiliating racial signs from the stores. On the basis of these promises Rev. Shuttlesworth and the leaders of the Alabama Christian Movement for Human Rights agreed to call a moratorium on any type of demonstrations. As the weeks and months unfolded we realized that we were the victims of a broken promise. The signs remained. Like so many experiences of the past we were confronted with blasted hopes, and the dark shadow of a deep disappointment settled upon us. So we had no alternative except that of preparing for direct action, whereby we would present our very bodies as a means of laying our case before the conscience of the local and national community. We were not unmindful of the difficulties involved. So we decided to go through a process of self-purification. We started having workshops on non-violence and repeatedly asked ourselves the questions, "Are you able to accept blows without retaliating?" "Are you able to endure the ordeals of jail?" We decided to set our direct action program around the Easter season, realizing that with the exception of Christmas, this was the largest shopping period of the year. Knowing that a strong economic withdrawal program would be the by-product of direct action, we felt that this was the best time to bring pressure on the merchants for the needed changes. Then it occurred to us that the March election was ahead and so we speedily decided to postpone action until after election day. When we discovered that Mr. Connor was in the run-off, we decided again to postpone action so that the demonstrations could not be used to cloud the issues. At this time we agreed to begin our nonviolent witness the day after the run-off.

This reveals that we did not move irresponsibly into direct action. We too wanted to see Mr. Connor defeated; so we went through postponement after postponement to aid in this community need. After this we felt that direct action could be delayed no longer.

You may well ask, "Why direct action? Why sit-ins, marches, etc.? Isn't negotiation a better path?" You are exactly right in your call for negotiation. Indeed, this is the purpose of direct action. Nonviolent direct action seeks to create such a crisis and establish such creative tension that a community that has constantly refused to negotiate is forced to confront the issue. It seeks so to dramatize the issue that it can no longer be ignored. I just referred to the creation of tension as a part of the work of the nonviolent resister. This may sound rather shocking. But I must confess that I am not afraid of the word tension. I have earnestly worked and preached against violent tension, but there is a type of constructive nonviolent tension that is necessary for growth. Just as Socrates felt that it was necessary to create a tension in the mind so that individuals could rise from the bondage of myths and half-truths to the unfettered realm of creative analysis and objective appraisal, we must see the need of having nonviolent gadflies to create the kind of tension in society that will help men to rise from the dark depths of prejudice and racism to the majestic heights of understanding and brotherhood. So the purpose of the direct action is to create a situation so crisis-packed that it will inevitably open the door to negotiation. We, therefore, concur with you in your call for negotiation. Too long has our beloved Southland been bogged down in the tragic attempt to live in monologue rather than dialogue.

One of the basic points in your statement is that our acts are untimely. Some have asked, "Why didn't you give the new administration time to act?" The only answer that I can give to this inquiry is that the new administration must be prodded about as much as the outgoing one before its acts. We will be sadly mistaken if we feel that the election of Mr. Boutwell will bring the millennium to Birmingham. While Mr. Boutwell is much more articulate and gentle than Mr. Connor, they are both segregationists, dedicated to the task of maintaining the status quo. The hope I see in Mr. Boutwell is that he will be reasonable enough to see the futility of massive resistance to desegregation. But he will not see this without pressure from the devotees of civil rights. My

friends, I must say to you that we have not made a single gain in
civil rights without determined legal and nonviolent pressure. History is the long and tragic story of the fact that privileged groups
seldom give up their privileges voluntarily. Individuals may see
the moral light and voluntarily give up their unjust posture; but
as Reinhold Niebuhr has reminded us, groups are more immoral
than individuals.

We know through painful experience that freedom is never voluntarily given by the oppressor; it must be demanded by the oppressed. Frankly, I have never yet engaged in a direct action movement that was "well timed," according to the timetable of those
who have not suffered unduly from the disease of segregation. For
years now I have heard the words "Wait!" It rings in the ear of
every Negro with a piercing familiarity. This "Wait" has almost
always meant "Never." It has been a tranquilizing thalidomide, re-
lieving the emotional stress for a moment, only to give birth to an
ill-formed infant of frustration. We must come to see with the distinguished jurist of yesterday that "justice too long delayed is justice denied." We have waited for more than three hundred and
forty years for our constitutional and God-given rights. The nations
of Asia and Africa are moving with jet-like speed toward the goal
of political independence, and we still creep at horse and buggy
pace toward the gaining of a cup of coffee at a lunch counter. I
guess it is easy for those who have never felt the stinging darts of
segregation to say, "Wait." But when you have seen vicious mobs
lynch your mothers and fathers at will and drown your sisters and
brothers at whim; when you have seen hate-filled policemen curse,
kick, brutalize and even kill your black brothers and sisters with
impunity; when you see the vast majority of your twenty million
Negro brothers smothering in an air-tight cage of poverty in the
midst of an affluent society; when you suddenly find your tongue
twisted and your speech stammering as you seek to explain to your
six-year-old daughter why she can't go to the public amusement
park that has just been advertised on television, and see tears well-
ing up in her little eyes when she is told that Funtown is closed to
colored children, and see the depressing clouds of inferiority begin
to form in her little mental sky, and see her begin to distort her
little personality by unconsciously developing a bitterness toward

white people; when you have to concoct an answer for a five-year-old son asking in agonizing pathos: "Daddy, why do white people treat colored people so mean?"; when you take a cross country drive and find it necessary to sleep night after night in the uncomfortable corners of your automobile because no motel will accept you; when you are humiliated day in and day out by nagging signs reading "white" and "colored"; when your first name becomes "nigger" and your middle name becomes "boy" (however old you are) and your last name becomes "John," and when your wife and mother are never given the respected title "Mrs."; when you are harried by day and haunted at night by the fact that you are a Negro, living constantly at tip-toe stance never quite knowing what to expect next, and plagued with inner fears and outer resentments; when you are forever fighting a degenerating sense of "nobodiness"; then you will understand why we find it difficult to wait. There comes a time when the cup of endurance runs over, and men are no longer willing to be plunged into an abyss of injustice where they experience the blackness of corroding despair. I hope, sirs, you can understand our legitimate and unavoidable impatience.

You express a great deal of anxiety over our willingness to break laws. This is certainly a legitimate concern. Since we so diligently urge people to obey the Supreme Court's decision of 1954 outlawing segregation in the public schools, it is rather strange and paradoxical to find us consciously breaking laws. One may well ask, "How can you advocate breaking some laws and obeying others?" The answer is found in the fact that there are two types of laws: There are *just* and there are *unjust* laws. I would agree with Saint Augustine that "An unjust law is no law at all."

Now what is the difference between the two? How does one determine when a law is just or unjust? A just law is a man-made code that squares with the moral law or the law of God. An unjust law is a code that is out of harmony with the moral law. To put it in the terms of Saint Thomas Aquinas, an unjust law is a human law that is not rooted in eternal and natural law. Any law that uplifts human personality is just. Any law that degrades human personality is unjust. All segregation statutes are unjust because segregation distorts the soul and damages the personality. It gives the segregator a false sense of superiority, and the segregated a false sense of inferiority. To use the words of Martin Buber, the great Jewish philosopher, segregation substitutes an "I-it" relationship for the "I-thou" relationship, and ends up relegating persons to the status of things. So segregation is not only politically, economically and sociologically unsound, but it is morally wrong and sinful. Paul Tillich has said that sin is separation. Isn't segregation an existential expression of man's tragic separation, an expression of his awful estrangement, his terrible sinfulness? So I can urge men to disobey segregation ordinances because they are morally wrong.

Let us turn to a more concrete example of just and unjust laws. An unjust law is a code that a majority inflicts on a minority that is not binding on itself. This is difference made legal. On the other hand a just law is a code that a majority compels a minority to follow that it is willing to follow itself. This is sameness made legal.

Let me give another explanation. An unjust law is a code inflicted upon a minority which that minority had no part in enacting or creating because they did not have the unhampered right to vote. Who can say that the legislature of Alabama which set up the segregation laws was democratically elected? Throughout the state of Alabama all types of conniving methods are used to prevent Negroes from becoming registered voters and there are some counties without a single Negro registered to vote despite the fact that the Negro constitutes a majority of the population. Can any law set up in such a state be considered democratically structured?

These are just a few examples of unjust and just laws. There are some instances when a law is just on its face and unjust in its application. For instance, I was arrested Friday on a charge of parading without a permit. Now there is nothing wrong with an ordinance which requires a permit for a parade, but when the ordinance is used to preserve segregation and to deny citizens the First Amendment privilege of peaceful assembly and peaceful protest, then it becomes unjust.

I hope you can see the distinction I am trying to point out. In no sense do I advocate evading or defying the law as the rabid segregationist would do. This would lead to anarchy. One who breaks an unjust law must do it *openly, lovingly* (not hatefully as the white mothers did in New Orleans when they were seen on television screaming "nigger, nigger, nigger"), and with a willingness to accept the penalty. I submit that an individual who breaks a law that conscience tells him is unjust, and willingly accepts the penalty by staying in jail to arouse the conscience of the community over its injustice, is in reality expressing the very highest respect for law.

Of course, there is nothing new about this kind of civil disobedience. It was seen sublimely in the refusal of Shadrach, Meshach and Abednego to obey the laws of Nebuchadnezzar because a higher moral law was involved. It was practiced superbly by the early Christians who were willing to face hungry lions and the excruciating pain of chopping blocks, before submitting to certain unjust laws of the Roman empire. To a degree academic freedom is a reality today because Socrates practiced civil disobedience.

We can never forget that everything Hitler did in Germany was "legal" and everything the Hungarian freedom fighters did in Hungary was "illegal." It was "illegal" to aid and comfort a Jew in Hitler's Germany. But I am sure that if I had lived in Germany during that time I would have aided and comforted my Jewish brothers even though it was illegal. If I lived in a Communist country today where certain principles dear to the Christian faith are suppressed, I believe I would openly advocate disobeying these anti-religious laws. I must make two honest confessions to you, my Christian and Jewish brothers. First, I must confess that over the last few years I have been gravely disappointed with the white moderate. I have almost reached the regrettable conclusion that the Negro's great stumbling block in the stride toward freedom is not the White Citizen's Council-er or the Ku Klux Klanner, but the white moderate who is more devoted to "order" than to justice; who prefers a negative peace which is the absence of tension to a positive peace which is the presence of justice; who constantly says, "I agree with you in the goal you seek, but I can't agree with your methods of direct action"; who paternalistically feels that he can set the timetable for another man's freedom; who lives by the myth of time and who constantly advises the Negro to wait until a "more convenient season." Shallow understanding from people of goodwill is more frustrating than absolute misunderstanding from people of ill will. Lukewarm acceptance is much more bewildering than outright rejection.

I had hoped that the white moderate would understand that law and order exist for the purpose of establishing justice, and that when they fail to do this they become dangerously structured dams that block the flow of social progress. I had hoped that the white moderate would understand that the present tension of the South is merely a necessary phase of the transition from an obnoxious negative peace, where the Negro passively accepted his unjust plight, to a substance-filled positive peace, where all men will respect the dignity and worth of human personality. Actually, we who engage in nonviolent direct action are not the creators of tension. We merely bring to the surface the hidden tension that is already alive. We bring it out in the open where it can be seen and dealt with. Like a boil that can never be cured as long as it is covered up but must be opened with all its pus-flowing ugliness to the natural medicines of air and light, injustice must likewise be exposed, with all of the tension its exposing creates, to the light of human conscience and the air of national opinion before it can be cured.

In your statement you asserted that our actions, even though peaceful, must be condemned because they precipitate violence. But can this assertion be logically made? Isn't this like condemning the robbed man because his possession of money precipitated the evil act of robbery? Isn't this like condemning Socrates because his unswerving commitment to truth and his philosophical delvings precipitated the misguided popular mind to make him drink the hemlock? Isn't this like condemning Jesus because His unique God-Consciousness and never-ceasing devotion to His will precipitated the evil act of crucifixion? We must come to see, as federal courts have consistently affirmed, that it is immoral to urge an individual to withdraw his efforts to gain his basic constitutional rights because the quest precipitates violence. Society must protect the robbed and punish the robber.

I had also hoped that the white moderate would reject the myth of time. I received a letter this morning from a white brother in Texas which said: "All Christians know that the colored people will receive equal rights eventually, but it is possible that you are in too great of a religious hurry. It has taken Christianity almost 2000 years to accomplish what it has. The teachings of Christ take time to come to earth." All that is said here grows out of a tragic misconception of time. It is the strangely irrational notion that there is something in the very flow of time that will inevitably cure all ills. Actually time is neutral. It can be used either destructively or constructively. I am coming to feel that the people of ill will have used time much more effectively than the people of goodwill. We will have to repent in this generation not merely for the vitriolic words and actions of the bad people, but for the appalling silence of the good people. We must come to see that human progress never rolls in on wheels of inevitability. It comes through the tireless efforts and persistent work of men willing to be co-workers with God, and without this hard work time itself becomes an ally of the forces of social stagnation. We must use time creatively, and forever realize that the time is always ripe to do right. Now is the time to make real the promise of democracy, and transform our pending national elegy into a creative psalm of brotherhood. Now is the time to lift our national policy from the quicksand of racial injustice to the solid rock of human dignity.

You spoke of our activity in Birmingham as extreme. At first I was rather disappointed that fellow clergymen would see my nonviolent efforts as those of the extremist. I started thinking about the fact that I stand in the middle of two opposing forces in the Negro community. One is a force of complacency made up of Negroes who, as a result of long years of oppression, have been so completely drained of self-respect and a sense of "somebodiness" that they have adjusted to segregation, and, of a few Negroes in the middle class who, because of a degree of academic and economic security, and because at points they profit by segregation, have unconsciously become insensitive to the problems of the masses. The other force is one of bitterness and hatred, and comes perilously close to advocating violence. It is expressed in the various black nationalist groups that are springing up over the nation, the largest and best known being Elijah Muhammad's Muslim movement. This movement is nourished by the contemporary frustration over the continued existence of racial discrimination. It is made up of people who have lost faith in America, who have absolutely repudiated Christianity, and who have concluded that the white man is an incurable "devil." I have tried to stand between these two forces, saying that we need not follow the "do-nothingism" of the complacent or the hatred and despair of the black nationalist. There is the more excellent way of love and non-violent protest. I'm grateful to God that, through the Negro church, the dimension of nonviolence entered our struggle. If this philosophy had not emerged, I am convinced that by now many streets of the South would be flowing with floods of blood. And I am further convinced that if our white brothers dismiss as "rabble rousers" and "outside agitators" those of us who are working through the channels of nonviolent direct action and refuse to support our nonviolent efforts, millions of Negroes, out of frustration and despair, will seek solace and security in black nationalist ideologies, a development that will lead inevitably to a frightening racial nightmare.

Oppressed people cannot remain oppressed forever. The urge for freedom will eventually come. This is what happened to the American Negro. Something within has reminded him of his birthright of freedom; something without has reminded him that he can gain it. Consciously and unconsciously, he has been swept in by what the Germans call the *Zeitgeist*, and with his black brothers of Africa, and his brown and yellow brothers of Asia, South America and the Caribbean, he is moving with a sense of cosmic urgency toward the promised land of racial justice. Recognizing this vital urge that has engulfed the Negro community, one should readily understand public demonstrations. The Negro has many pent-up resentments and latent frustrations. He has to get them out. So let him march sometime; let him have his prayer pilgrimages to the city hall; understand why he must have sit-ins and freedom rides. If his repressed emotions do not come out in these nonviolent ways, they will come out in ominous expressions of violence. This is not a threat; it is a fact of history. So I have not said to my people "get rid of your discontent." But I have tried to say that this normal and healthy discontent can be channelized through the creative outlet of nonviolent direct action. Now this approach is being dismissed as extremist. I must admit that I was initially disappointed in being so categorized.

But as I continued to think about the matter I gradually gained a bit of satisfaction from being considered an extremist. Was not

Jesus an extremist in love—"Love your enemies, bless them that curse you, pray for them that despitefully use you." Was not Amos an extremist for justice—"Let justice roll down like waters and righteousness like a mighty stream." Was not Paul an extremist for the gospel of Jesus Christ—"I bear in my body the marks of the Lord Jesus." Was not Martin Luther an extremist—"Here I stand; I can do none other so help me God." Was not John Bunyan an extremist—"I will stay in jail to the end of my days before I make a butchery of my conscience." Was not Abraham Lincoln an extremist—"This nation cannot survive half slave and half free." Was not Thomas Jefferson an extremist—"We hold these truths to be self-evident, that all men are created equal." So the question is not whether we will be extremist but what kind of extremist will we be. Will we be extremists for hate or will we be extremists for love? Will we be extremists for the preservation of injustice—or will we be extremists for the cause of justice? In that dramatic scene on Calvary's hill, three men were crucified. We must not forget that all three were crucified for the same crime—the crime of extremism. Two were extremists for immorality, and thusly fell below their environment. The other, Jesus Christ, was an extremist for love, truth and goodness, and thereby rose above his environment. So, after all, maybe the South, the nation and the world are in dire need of creative extremists.

I had hoped that the white moderate would see this. Maybe I was too optimistic. Maybe I expected too much. I guess I should have realized that few members of a race that has oppressed another race can understand or appreciate the deep groans and passionate yearnings of those that have been oppressed and still fewer have the vision to see that injustice must be rooted out by strong, persistent and determined action. I am thankful, however, that some of our white brothers have grasped the meaning of this social revolution and committed themselves to it. They are still all too small in quantity, but they are big in quality. Some like Ralph McGill, Lillian Smith, Harry Golden and James Dabbs have written about our struggle in eloquent, prophetic and understanding terms. Others have marched with us down nameless streets of the South. They have languished in filthy roach-infested jails, suffering the abuse and brutality of angry policemen who see them as "dirty nigger lovers." They, unlike so many of their moderate brothers and sisters, have recognized the urgency of the moment and sensed the need for powerful "action" antidotes to combat the disease of segregation.

Let me rush on to mention my other disappointment. I have been so greatly disappointed with the white church and its leadership. Of course, there are some notable exceptions. I am not unmindful of the fact that each of you has taken some significant stands on this issue. I commend you, Rev. Stallings, for your Christian stand on this past Sunday, in welcoming Negroes to your worship service on a non-segregated basis. I commend the Catholic leaders of this state for integrating Springhill College several years ago.

But despite these notable exceptions I must honestly reiterate that I have been disappointed with the church. I do not say that as one of the negative critics who can always find something wrong with the church. I say it as a minister of the gospel, who loves the church; who was nurtured in its bosom; who has been sustained by its spiritual blessings and who will remain true to it as long as the cord of life shall lengthen.

I had the strange feeling when I was suddenly catapulted into the leadership of the bus protest in Montgomery several years ago that we would have the support of the white church. I felt that the white ministers, priests and rabbis of the South would be some of our strongest allies. Instead, some have been outright opponents, refusing to understand the freedom movement and misrepresenting its leaders; all too many others have been more cautious than courageous and have remained silent behind the anesthetizing security of the stained-glass windows.

In spite of my shattered dreams of the past, I came to Birmingham with the hope that the white religious leadership of this community would see the justice of our cause, and with deep moral concern, serve as the channel through which our just grievances would get to the power structure. I had hoped that each of you would understand. But again I have been disappointed. I have heard numerous religious leaders of the South call upon their worshippers to comply with a desegregation decision because it is the *law*, but I have longed to hear white ministers say, "Follow this decree because integration is morally *right* and the Negro is your brother." In the midst of blatant injustices inflicted upon the Negro, I have watched white churches stand on the sideline and merely mouth pious irrelevancies and sanctimonious trivialities. In the midst of a mighty struggle to rid our nation of racial and economic injustice, I have heard so many ministers say, "Those are social issues with which the gospel has no real concern," and I have watched so many churches commit themselves to a completely other-worldly religion which made a strange distinction between body and soul, the sacred and the secular.

So here we are moving toward the exit of the twentieth century with a religious community largely adjusted to the status quo, standing as a tail-light behind other community agencies rather than a headlight leading men to higher levels of justice.

I have traveled the length and breadth of Alabama, Mississippi and all the other southern states. On sweltering summer days and crisp autumn mornings I have looked at her beautiful churches with their lofty spires pointing heavenward. I have beheld the impressive outlay of her massive religious education buildings. Over and over again I have found myself asking: "What kind of people worship here? Who is their God? Where were their voices when the lips of Governor Barnett dripped with words of interposition and nullification? Where were they when Governor Wallace gave the clarion call for defiance and hatred? Where were their voices of support when tired, bruised and weary Negro men and women decided to rise from the dark dungeons of complacency to the bright hills of creative protest?"

Yes, these questions are still in my mind. In deep disappointment, I have wept over the laxity of the church. But be assured that my tears have been tears of love. There can be no deep disappointment where there is not deep love. Yes, I love the church; I love her sacred walls. How could I do otherwise? I am in the rather unique position of being the son, the grandson and the great-grandson of preachers. Yes, I see the church as the body of Christ. But, oh! How we have blemished and scarred that body through social neglect and fear of being nonconformists.

There was a time when the church was very powerful. It was during that period when the early Christians rejoiced when they were deemed worthy to suffer for what they believed. In those days the church was not merely a thermometer that recorded the ideas and principles of popular opinion; it was a thermostat that transformed the mores of society. Wherever the early Christians entered a town the power structure got disturbed and immediately sought to convict them for being "disturbers of the peace" and "outside agitators." But they went on with the conviction that they were "a colony of heaven," and had to obey God rather than man. They were small in number but big in commitment. They were too God-intoxicated to be "astronomically intimidated." They brought an end to such ancient evils as infanticide and gladiatorial contest.

Things are different now. The contemporary church is often a weak, ineffectual voice with an uncertain sound. It is so often the arch supporter of the status quo. Far from being disturbed by the presence of the church, the power structure of the average community is consoled by the church's silent and often vocal sanction of things as they are.

But the judgment of God is upon the church as never before. If the church of today does not recapture the sacrificial spirit of the early church, it will lose its authentic ring, forfeit the loyalty of millions, and be dismissed as an irrelevant social club with no meaning for the twentieth century. I am meeting young people every day whose disappointment with the church has risen to outright disgust.

Maybe again, I have been too optimistic. Is organized religion too inextricably bound to the status quo to save our nation and the world? Maybe I must turn my faith to the inner spiritual church, the church within the church, as the true *ecclesia* and the hope of the world. But again I am thankful to God that some noble souls from the ranks of organized religion have broken loose from the paralyzing chains of conformity and joined us as active partners in the struggle for freedom. They have left their secure congregations and walked the streets of Albany, Georgia, with us. They have gone through the highways of the South on tortuous rides for freedom. Yes, they have gone to jail with us. Some have been kicked out of their churches, and lost support of their bishops and fellow ministers. But they have gone with the faith that right defeated is stronger than evil triumphant. These men have been the leaven in the lump of the race. Their witness has been the spiritual salt that has preserved the true meaning of the Gospel in these troubled times. They have carved a tunnel of hope through the dark mountain of disappointment.

I hope the church as a whole will meet the challenge of this decisive hour. But even if the church does not come to the aid of justice, I have no despair about the future. I have no fear about the outcome of our struggle in Birmingham, even if our motives are presently misunderstood. We will reach the goal of freedom in Birmingham and all over the nation, because the goal of America is freedom. Abused and scorned though we may be, our destiny is tied up with the destiny of America. Before the pilgrims landed at Plymouth we were here. Before the pen of Jefferson etched across the pages of history the majestic words of the Declaration of Independence, we were here. For more than two centuries our fore-parents labored in this country without wages; they made cotton king; and they built the homes of their masters in the midst of brutal injustice and shameful humiliation—and yet out of a bottomless vitality they continued to thrive and develop. If the inexpressible cruelties of slavery could not stop us, the opposition we now face will surely fail. We will win our freedom because the sacred heritage of our nation and the eternal will of God are embodied in our echoing demands.

I must close now. But before closing I am impelled to mention one other point in your statement that troubled me profoundly. You warmly commended the Birmingham police force for keeping "order" and "preventing violence." I don't believe you would have so warmly commended the police force if you had seen its angry violent dogs literally biting six unarmed, nonviolent Negroes. I don't believe you would so quickly commend the policemen if you would observe their ugly and inhuman treatment of Negroes here in the city jail; if you would watch them push and curse old Negro women and young Negro girls; if you would see them slap and kick old Negro men and young boys; if you will observe them, as they did on two occasions, refuse to give us food because we wanted to sing our grace together. I'm sorry that I can't join you in your praise for the police department.

It is true that they have been rather disciplined in their public handling of the demonstrators. In this sense they have been rather publicly "nonviolent." But for what purpose? To preserve the evil system of segregation. Over the last few years I have consistently preached that nonviolence demands that the means we use must be as pure as the ends we seek. So I have tried to make it clear that it is wrong to use immoral means to attain moral ends. But now I must affirm that it is just as wrong, or even more so, to use moral means to preserve immoral ends. Maybe Mr. Connor and his policemen have been rather publicly nonviolent, as Chief Pritchett was in Albany, Georgia, but they have used the moral means of nonviolence to maintain the immoral end of flagrant racial injustice. T. S. Eliot has said that there is no greater treason than to do the right deed for the wrong reason.

I wish you had commended the Negro sit-inners and demonstrators of Birmingham for their sublime courage, their willingness to suffer and their amazing discipline in the midst of the most inhuman provocation. One day the South will recognize its real heroes. They will be the James Merediths, courageously and with a majestic sense of purpose facing jeering and hostile mobs and the agonizing loneliness that characterizes the life of the pioneer. They will be old, oppressed, battered Negro women, symbolized in a seventy-two year old woman of Montgomery, Alabama, who rose up with a sense of dignity and with her people decided not to ride the segregated buses, and responded to one who inquired about her tiredness with ungrammatical profundity: "My feet is tired, but my soul is rested." They will be the young high school and college students, young ministers of the Gospel and a host of their elders courageously and nonviolently sitting-in at lunch counters and willingly going to jail for conscience's sake. One day the South will know that when these disinherited children of God sat down at lunch counters they were in reality standing up for the best in the American dream and the most sacred values in our Judeo-Christian heritage, and thusly, carrying our while nation back to those great wells of democracy which were dug deep by the founding fathers in the formulation of the Constitution and the Declaration of Independence.

Never before have I written a letter this long (or should I say a book?). I'm afraid that it is much too long to take your precious time. I can assure you that it would have been much shorter if I had been writing from a comfortable desk, but what else is there to do when you are alone for days in the dull monotony of a narrow jail cell other than write long letters, think strange thoughts, and pray long prayers?

If I have said anything in this letter that is an overstatement of the truth and is indicative of an unreasonable impatience, I beg you to forgive me. If I have said anything in this letter that is an understatement of the truth and is indicative of my having a patience that makes me patient with anything less than brotherhood, I beg God to forgive me.

I hope this letter finds you strong in the faith. I also hope that circumstances will soon make it possible for me to meet each of you, not as an integrationist or a civil-rights leader, but as a fellow clergyman and a Christian brother. Let us all hope that the dark clouds of racial prejudice will soon pass away and the deep fog of misunderstanding will be lifted from our fear-drenched communities and in some not too distant tomorrow the radiant stars of love and brotherhood will shine over our great nation with all of their scintillating beauty.

Yours for the cause of Peace and Brotherhood,
Martin Luther King, Jr.

JOHN RAWLS

The Justification of Civil Disobedience

I. Introduction

I should like to discuss briefly, and in an informal way, the grounds of civil disobedience in a constitutional democracy. Thus, I shall limit my remarks to the conditions under which we may, by civil disobedience, properly oppose legally established democratic authority; I am not concerned with the situation under other kinds of government nor, except incidentally, with other forms of resistance. My thought is that in a reasonably just (though of course not perfectly just) democratic regime civil disobedience, when it is justified, is normally to be understood as a political action which addresses the sense of justice of the majority in order to urge reconsideration of the measures protested and to warn that in the firm opinion of the dissenters the conditions of social cooperation are not being honored. This characterization of civil disobedience is intended to apply to dissent on fundamental questions of internal policy, a limitation which I shall follow to simplify our question.

II. The Social Contract Doctrine

It is obvious that the justification of civil disobedience depends upon the theory of political duty in general and so we may appropriately begin with a few comments on this question. The two chief virtues of social institutions are justice and efficiency, where by the

"The Justification of Civil Disobedience" by John Rawls. This article was originally presented at the meetings of the American Political Science Association, September 1966. Some revisions have been made and two paragraphs have been added to the last section. Printed by permission of the author.

efficiency of institutions I understand their effectiveness for certain social conditions and ends the fulfillment of which is to every one's advantage. We should comply with and do our part in just and efficient social arrangements for at least two reasons: first of all, we have a natural duty not to oppose the establishment of just and efficient institutions (when they do not yet exist) and to uphold and comply with them (when they do exist); and second, assuming that we have knowingly accepted the benefits of these institutions and plan to continue to do so, and that we have encouraged and expect others to do their part, we also have an obligation to do our share when, as the arrangement requires, it comes our turn. Thus, we often have both a natural duty as well as an obligation to support just and efficient institutions, the obligation arising from our voluntary acts while the duty does not.

Now all this is perhaps obvious enough, but it does not take us very far. Any more particular conclusions depend upon the conception of justice which is the basis of a theory of political duty. I believe that the appropriate conception, at least for an account of political duty in a constitutional democracy, is that of the social contract theory from which so much of our political thought derives. If we are careful to interpret it in a suitably general way, I hold that this doctrine provides a satisfactory basis for political theory, indeed even for ethical theory itself, but this is beyond our present concern.[1] The interpretation I suggest is the following: that the principles to which social arrangements must conform, and in particular the principles of justice, are those which free and rational men would agree to in an original position of equal liberty; and similarly, the principles which govern men's relations to institutions and define their natural duties and obligations are the principles to which they would consent when so situated. It should be noted straightway that in this interpretation of the contract theory the principles of justice are understood as the outcome of a hypothetical agreement. They are principles which would be agreed to if the situation of the original position were to arise. There is no mention

1. By the social contract theory I have in mind the doctrine found in Locke, Rousseau, and Kant, I have attempted to give an interpretation of this view in: "Justice as Fairness", *Philosophical Review* (April, 1958) and "Justice and Constitutional Liberty", *Nomos* VI (1963).

of an actual agreement nor need such an agreement even be made. Social arrangements are just or unjust according to whether they accord with the principles for assigning and securing fundamental rights and liberties which would be chosen in the original position. This position is, to be sure, the analytic analogue of the traditional notion of the state of nature, but it must not be mistaken for a historical occasion. Rather it is a hypothetical situation which embodies the basic ideas of the contract doctrine; the description of this situation enables us to work out which principles would be adopted. I must now say something about these matters.

The contract doctrine has always supposed that the persons in the original position have equal powers and rights, that is, that they are symmetrically situated with respect to any arrangements for reaching agreement, and that coalitions and the like are excluded. But it is also an essential element (which has not been sufficiently observed although it is implicit in Kant's version of the theory) that there are very strong restrictions on what the contractees are presumed to know. In particular, I interpret the theory to hold that the parties do not know their position in society, past, present, or future; nor do they know which institutions exist. Again, they do not know their own place in the distribution of natural talents and abilities, whether they are intelligent or strong, man or woman, and so on. Finally, they do not know their own particular interests and preferences or the system of ends which they wish to advance: they do not know their conception of the good. In all these respects the parties are confronted with a veil of ignorance which prevents any one from being able to take advantage of his good fortune or particular interests or from being disadvantaged by them. What the parties do know (or assume) is that Hume's circumstances of justice obtain: namely, that the bounty of nature is not so generous as to render cooperative schemes superfluous nor so harsh as to make them impossible. Moreover, they assume that the extent of their altruism is limited and that, in general, they do not take an interest in one another's interests. Thus, given the special features of the original position, each man tries to do the best he can for himself by insisting on principles calculated to protect and advance his system of ends whatever it turns out to be.

I believe that as a consequence of the peculiar nature of the original position there would be an agreement on the following two principles for assigning rights and duties and for regulating distributive shares as these are determined by the fundamental institutions of society: first, each person is to have an equal right to the most extensive liberty compatible with a like liberty for all; and second, social and economic inequalities (as defined by the institutional structure or fostered by it) are to be arranged so that they are both to everyone's advantage and attached to positions and offices open to all. In view of the content of these two principles and their application to the main institutions of society, and therefore to the social system as a whole, we may regard them as the two principles of justice. Basic social arrangements are just insofar as they conform to these principles; and we can, if we like, discuss questions of justice directly by reference to them. But a deeper understanding of the justification of civil disobedience requires, I think, an account of the derivation of these principles provided by the doctrine of the social contract. Part of our task is to show why this is so.

III. The Grounds of Compliance with an Unjust Law

If we assume that in the original position men would agree both to the principle of doing their part when they have accepted and plan to continue to accept the benefits of just institutions (the principle of fairness), and also to the principle of not preventing the establishment of just institutions and of upholding and complying with them when they do exist, then the contract doctrine easily accounts for our having to conform to just institutions. But how does it account for the fact that we are normally required to comply with unjust laws as well? The injustice of a law is not a sufficient ground for not complying with it any more than the legal validity of legislation is always sufficient to require obedience to it. Sometimes one hears these extremes asserted, but I think that we need not take them seriously.

An answer to our question can be given by elaborating the social contract theory in the following way. I interpret it to hold that one is to envisage a series of agreements as follows: first, men are to agree upon the principles of justice in the original position. Then they are to move to a constitutional convention in which they choose a constitution that satisfies the principles of justice already chosen. Finally they assume the role of a legislative body and guided by the principles of justice enact laws subject to the constraints and procedures of the just constitution. The decisions reached in any stage are binding in all subsequent stages. Now whereas in the original position the contractees have no knowledge of their society or of their own position in it, in both a constitutional convention and a legislature, they do know certain general facts about their institutions, for example, the statistics regarding employment and output required for fiscal and economic policy. But no one knows particular facts about his own social class or his place in the distribution of natural assets. On each occasion the contractees have the knowledge required to make their agreement rational from the appropriate point of view, but not so much as to make them prejudiced. They are unable to tailor principles and legislation to take advantage of their social or natural position; a veil of ignorance prevents their knowing what this position is. With this series of agreements in mind, we can characterize just laws and policies as those which would be enacted were this whole process correctly carried out.

In choosing a constitution the aim is to find among the just constitutions the one which is most likely, given the general facts about the society in question, to lead to just and effective legislation. The principles of justice provide a criterion for the laws desired: the problem is to find a set of political procedures that will give this outcome. I shall assume that, at least under the normal conditions of a modern state, the best constitution is some form of democratic regime affirming equal political liberty and using some sort of majority (or other plurality) rule. Thus it follows that on the contract theory a constitutional democracy of some sort is required by the principles of justice. At the same time it is essential to observe that the constitutional process is always a case of what we may call imperfect procedural justice: that is, there is no feasible political procedure which guarantees that the enacted legislation is just even though we have (let's suppose) a standard for just legislation. In simple cases, such as games of fair division, there are procedures which always lead to the right outcome (assume that equal shares is fair and let the man who cuts the cake take the last piece). These situations are those of perfect procedural justice. In other cases it does not matter what the outcome is as long as the fair procedure is followed: fairness of the process is transferred to the result (fair gambling is an instance of this). These situations are those of pure procedural justice. The constitutional process, like a criminal trial, resembles neither of these; the result matters and we have a standard for it. The difficulty is that we cannot frame a procedure which guarantees that only just and effective legislation is enacted. Thus even under a just constitution unjust laws may be passed and unjust policies enforced. Some form of the majority principle is necessary but the majority may be mistaken, more or less willfully, in what it legislates. In agreeing to a democratic constitution (as an instance of imperfect procedural justice) one accepts at the same time the principle of majority rule. Assuming that the constitution is just and that we have accepted and plan to continue to accept its benefits, we then have both an obligation and a natural duty (and in any case the duty) to comply with what the majority enacts even though it may be unjust. In this way we become bound to follow unjust laws, not always, of course, but provided the injustice does not exceed certain limits. We recognize that we must run the risk of suffering from the defects of one another's sense of justice; and this burden we are prepared to carry as long as it is more or less evenly distributed or does not weigh too heavily. Justice binds us to a just constitution and to the unjust laws which may be enacted under it in precisely the same way that it binds us to any other social arrangement. Once we take the sequence of stages into account, there is nothing unusual in our being required to comply with unjust laws.

It should be observed that the majority principle has a secondary place as a rule of procedure which is perhaps the most efficient one under usual circumstances for working a democratic constitution. The basis for it rests essentially upon the principles of justice and therefore we may, when conditions allow, appeal to these principles against unjust legislation. The justice of the constitution does not insure the justice of laws enacted under it; and while we often have both an obligation and a duty to comply with what the majority legislates (as long as it does not exceed certain limits), there is, of course, no corresponding obligation or duty to regard what the ma-

jority enacts as itself just. The right to make law does not guarantee that the decision is rightly made; and while the citizen submits in his conduct to the judgment of democratic authority, he
does not submit his judgment to it.[2] And if in his judgment the
enactments of the majority exceed certain bounds of injustice, the
citizen may consider civil disobedience. For we are not required to
accept the majority's acts unconditionally and to acquiesce in the
denial of our and others' liberties; rather we submit our conduct to
democratic authority to the extent necessary to share the burden of
working a constitutional regime distorted as it must inevitably be
by men's lack of wisdom and the defects of their sense of justice.

IV. The Place of Civil Disobedience
in a Constitutional Democracy

We are now in a position to say a few things about civil disobedience. I shall understand it to be a public, non violent, and
conscientious act contrary to law usually done with the intent to
bring about a change in the policies or laws of the government.[3]
Civil disobedience is a political act in the sense that it is an act
justified by moral principles which define a conception of civil society and the public good. It rests, then, on political conviction as
opposed to a search for self or group interest; and in the case of a
constitutional democracy, we may assume that this conviction involves the conception of justice (say that expressed by the contract
doctrine) which underlies the constitution itself. That is, in a viable
democratic regime there is a common conception of justice by reference to which its citizens regulate their political affairs and interpret
the constitution. Civil disobedience is a public act which the dissenter believes to be justified by this conception of justice and for
this reason it may be understood as addressing the sense of justice
of the majority in order to urge reconsideration of the measures
protested and to warn that, in the sincere opinion of the dissenters,
the conditions of social cooperation are not being honored: For the

2. On this point see A. E. Murphy's review of Yves Simon's The Philosophy
of Democratic Government (1951) in the Philosophical Review (April, 1952).
3. Here I follow H. A. Bedau's definition of civil disobedience. See his "On
Civil Disobedience," Journal of Philosophy (October, 1961).

principles of justice express precisely such conditions, and their persistent and deliberate violation in regard to basic liberties over any extended period of time cuts the ties of community and invites either submission or forceful resistance. By engaging in civil disobedience a minority leads the majority to consider whether it wants to have its acts taken in this way, or whether, in view of the common sense of justice, it wishes to acknowledge the claims of the minority.

Civil disobedience is also civil in another sense. Not only is it the outcome of a sincere conviction based on principles which regulate civic life, but it is public and non-violent, that is, it is done in a situation where arrest and punishment is expected and accepted without resistance. In this way it manifests a respect for legal procedures. Civil disobedience expresses disobedience to law within the limits of fidelity to law, and this feature of it helps to establish in the eyes of the majority that it is indeed conscientious and sincere, that it really is meant to address their sense of justice.[4] Being completely open about one's acts and being willing to accept the legal consequences of one's conduct is a bond given to make good one's sincerity, for that one's deeds are conscientious is not easy to demonstrate to another or even before oneself. No doubt it is possible to imagine a legal system in which conscientious belief that the law is unjust is accepted as a defense for non-compliance, and men of great honesty who are confident in one another might make such a system work. But as things are such a scheme would be unstable; we must pay a price in order to establish that we believe our actions have a moral basis in the convictions of the community.

The nonviolent nature of civil disobedience refers to the fact that it is intended to address the sense of justice of the majority and as such it is a form of speech, an expression of conviction. To engage in violent acts likely to injure and to hurt is incompatible with civil disobedience as a mode of address. Indeed, any interference with the basic rights of others tends to obscure the civilly disobedient quality of one's act. Civil disobedience is nonviolent in the further sense that the legal penalty for one's action is accepted and resistance is not (at least for the moment) contemplated. Non-

4. For a fuller discussion of this point to which I am indebted, see Charles Fried, "Moral Causation," *Harvard Law Review* (1964).

violence in this sense is to be distinguished from nonviolence as a religious or pacifist principle. While those engaging in civil disobedience have often held some such principle, there is no necessary connection between it and civil disobedience. For on the interpretation suggested, civil disobedience in a democratic society is best understood as an appeal to the principles of justice, the fundamental conditions of willing social cooperation among free men, which in the view of the community as a whole are expressed in the constitution and guide its interpretation. Being an appeal to the moral basis of public life, civil disobedience is a political and not primarily a religious act. It addresses itself to the common principles of justice which men can require one another to follow and not to the aspirations of love which they cannot. Moreover by taking part in civilly disobedient acts one does not foreswear indefinitely the idea of forceful resistance; for if the appeal against injustice is repeatedly denied, then the majority has declared its intention to invite submission or resistance and the latter may conceivably be justified even in a democratic regime. We are not required to acquiesce in the crushing of fundamental liberties by democratic majorities which have shown themselves blind to the principles of justice upon which justification of the constitution depends.

V. The Justification of Civil Disobedience

So far we have said nothing about the justification of civil disobedience, that is, the conditions under which civil disobedience may be engaged in consistent with the principles of justice that support a democratic regime. Our task is to see how the characterization of civil disobedience as addressed to the sense of justice of the majority (or to the citizens as a body) determines when such action is justified.

First of all, we may suppose that the normal political appeals to the majority have already been made in good faith and have been rejected, and that the standard means of redress have been tried. Thus, for example, existing political parties are indifferent to the claims of the minority and attempts to repeal the laws protested have been met with further repression since legal institutions are in the control of the majority. While civil disobedience should be recognized, I think, as a form of political action within the limits of fidelity to the rule of law, at the same time it is a rather desperate act just within these limits, and therefore it should, in general, be undertaken as a last resort when standard democratic processes have failed. In this sense it is not a normal political action. When it is justified there has been a serious breakdown; not only is there grave injustice in the law but a refusal more or less deliberate to correct it.

Second, since civil disobedience is a political act addressed to the sense of justice of the majority, it should usually be limited to substantial and clear violations of justice preferably to those which, if rectified, will establish a basis for doing away with remaining injustices. For this reason there is a presumption in favor of restricting civil disobedience to violations of the first principle of justice, the principle of equal liberty, and to barriers which contravene the second principle, the principle of open offices which protects equality of opportunity. It is not, of course, always easy to tell whether these principles are satisfied. But if we think of them as guaranteeing the fundamental equal political and civil liberties (including freedom of conscience and liberty of thought) and equality of opportunity, then it is often relatively clear whether their principles are being honored. After all, the equal liberties are defined by the visible structure of social institutions; they are to be incorporated into the recognized practice, if not the letter, of social arrangements. When minorities are denied the right to vote or to hold certain political offices, when certain religious groups are repressed and others denied equality of opportunity in the economy, this is often obvious and there is no doubt that justice is not being given. Whereas the first part of the second principle which requires that inequalities be to everyone's advantage is a much more imprecise and controversial matter. Not only is there a problem of assigning it a determinate and precise sense, but even if we do so and agree on what it should be, there is often a wide variety of reasonable opinion as to whether the principle is satisfied. The reason for this is that the principle applies primarily to fundamental economic and social policies. The choice of these depends upon theoretical and speculative beliefs as well as upon a wealth of concrete information, and all of this mixed with judgment and plain hunch, not to mention in actual cases prejudice and self-interest. Thus unless the laws of taxation are clearly designed to attack a basic equal liberty, they should not be protested by civil disobedience; the appeal to justice is not sufficiently clear and its resolution is best left to the political process. But violations of the equal liberties that define the common status of citizenship are another matter. The denial of these more or less deliberate over any extended period of time in the face of normal political protest is, in general, an appropriate object of civil disobedience. We may think of the social system as divided roughly into two parts, one which incorporates the fundamental equal liberties (including equality of opportunity) and another which embodies social and economic policies properly aimed at promoting the advantage of everyone. As a rule civil disobedience is best limited to the former where the appeal to justice is not only more definite and precise, but where, if it is effective, it tends to correct the injustices in the latter.

Third, civil disobedience should be restricted to those cases where the dissenter is willing to affirm that everyone else similarly subjected to the same degree of injustice has the right to protest in a similar way. That is, we must be prepared to authorize others to dissent in similar situations and in the same way, and to accept the consequences of their doing so. Thus, we may hold, for example, that the widespread disposition to disobey civilly clear violations of fundamental liberties more or less deliberate over an extended period of time would raise the degree of justice throughout society and would insure men's self-esteem as well as their respect for one another. Indeed, I believe this to be true, though certainly it is partly a matter of conjecture. As the contract doctrine emphasizes, since the principles of justice are principles which we would agree to in an original position of equality when we do not know our social position and the like, the refusal to grant justice is either the denial of the other as an equal (as one in regard to whom we are prepared to constrain our actions by principles which we would consent to) or the manifestation of a willingness to take advantage of natural contingencies and social fortune at his expense. In either case, injustice invites submission or resistance; but submission arouses the contempt of the oppressor and confirms him in his intention. If straightway, after a decent period of time to make reasonable political appeals in the normal way, men were in general to dissent by civil disobedience from infractions of the fundamental equal liberties, these liberties would, I believe, be more rather than less secure. Legitimate civil disobedience properly exercised is a stabilizing device in a constitutional regime tending to make it more firmly just.

Sometimes, however, there may be a complication in connection with this third condition. It is possible, although perhaps unlikely, that there are so many persons or groups with a sound case for resorting to civil disobedience (as judging by the foregoing criteria) that disorder would follow if they all did so. There might be serious injury to the just constitution. Or again, a group might be so large that some extra precaution is necessary in the extent to which its members organize and engage in civil disobedience. Theoretically the case is one in which a number of persons or groups are equally entitled to and all want to resort to civil disobedience, yet if they all do this, grave consequences for everyone may result. The question, then, is who among them may exercise their right, and it falls under the general problem of fairness. I cannot discuss the complexities of the matter here. Often a lottery or a rationing system can be set up to handle the case; but unfortunately the circumstances of civil disobedience rule out this solution. It suffices to note that a problem of fairness may arise and that those who contemplate civil disobedience should take it into account. They may have to reach an understanding as to who can exercise their right in the immediate situation and to recognize the need for special constraint.

The final condition, of a different nature, is the following. We have been considering when one has a right to engage in civil disobedience, and our conclusion is that one has this right should three conditions hold: when one is subject to injustice more or less deliberate over an extended period of time in the face of normal political protests; where the injustice is a clear violation of the liberties of equal citizenship; and provided that the general disposition to protest similarly in similar cases would have acceptable consequences. These conditions are not, I think, exhaustive but they seem to cover the more obvious points; yet even when they are satisfied and one has the right to engage in civil disobedience is still the different question of whether one should exercise this right, that is, whether by doing so one is likely to further one's ends. Having established one's right to protest one is then free to consider these tactical questions. We may be acting within our rights but still foolishly if our action only serves to provoke the harsh retaliation of the majority; and it is likely to do so if the majority lacks a sense of justice, or if the action is poorly timed or not well designed to make the appeal to the sense of justice effective. It is easy to think of instances of this sort, and in each case these practical questions have to be faced. From the standpoint of the theory of political duty we can only say that the exercise of the right should be rational and reasonably designed to advance the protestor's aims, and that weighing tactical questions presupposes that one has already established one's right, since tactical advantages in themselves do not support it.

VI. Conclusion: Several Objections Considered

In a reasonably affluent democratic society justice becomes the first virtue of institutions. Social arrangements irrespective of their efficiency must be reformed if they are significantly unjust. No increase in efficiency in the form of greater advantages for many justifies the loss of liberty of a few. That we believe this is shown by the fact that in a democracy the fundamental liberties of citizenship are not understood as the outcome of political bargaining nor are they subject to the calculus of social interests. Rather these liberties are fixed points which serve to limit political transactions and which determine the scope of calculations of social advantage. It is this fundamental place of the equal liberties which makes their systematic violation over any extended period of time a proper object of civil disobedience. For to deny men these rights is to infringe the conditions of social cooperation among free and rational persons, a fact which is evident to the citizens of a constitutional regime since it follows from the principles of justice which underlies their institutions. The justification of civil disobedience rests on the priority of justice and the equal liberties which it guarantees.

It is natural to object to this view of civil disobedience that it relies too heavily upon the existence of a sense of justice. Some may hold that the feeling for justice is not a vital political force, and that what moves men are various other interests, the desire for wealth, power, prestige, and so on. Now this is a large question the answer to which is highly conjectural and each tends to have his own opinion. But there are two remarks which may clarify what I have said: first, I have assumed that there is in a constitutional regime a common sense of justice the principles of which are recognized to support the constitution and to guide its interpretation. In any given situation particular men may be tempted to violate these principles, but the collective force in their behalf is usually effective since they are seen as the necessary terms of cooperation among free men; and presumably the citizens of a democracy (or sufficiently many of them) want to see justice done. Where these assumptions fail, the justifying conditions for civil disobedience (the first three) are not affected, but the rationality of engaging in it certainly is. In this case, unless the costs of repressing civil dissent injure the economic self-interest (or whatsoever) of the majority, protest may simply make the position of the minority worse. No doubt as a tactical matter civil disobedience is more effective when its appeal coincides with other interests, but a constitutional regime is not viable in the long run without an attachment to the principles of justice of the sort which we have assumed.

Then, further, there may be a misapprehension about the manner in which a sense of justice manifests itself. There is a tendency to think that it is shown by professions of the relevant principles together with actions of an altruistic nature requiring a considerable degree of self-sacrifice. But these conditions are obviously too strong, for the majority's sense of justice may show itself simply in its being unable to undertake the measures required to suppress the minority and to punish as the law requires the various acts of civil disobedience. The sense of justice undermines the will to uphold unjust institutions, and so a majority despite its superior power may give way. It is unprepared to force the minority to be subject to injustice. Thus, although the majority's action is reluctant and grudging, the role of the sense of justice is nevertheless essential, for without it the majority would have been willing to enforce the law and to defend its position. Once we see the sense of justice as working in this negative way to make established injustices indefensible, then it is recognized as a central element of democratic politics.

Finally, it may be objected that this account does not settle the question of who is to say when the situation is such as to justify civil disobedience. And because it does not answer this question, it invites anarchy by encouraging every man to decide the matter for himself. Now the reply to this is that each man must indeed settle this question for himself, although he may, of course, decide wrongly. This is true on any theory of political duty and obligation, at least on any theory compatible with the principles of a democratic constitution. The citizen is responsible for what he does. If we ordinarily think that we should comply with the law, this is because our political principles normally lead to this conclusion. There is a presumption in favor of compliance in the absence of good reasons to the contrary. But because each man is responsible and must decide for himself as best he can whether the circumstances justify civil disobedience, it does not follow that he may decide as he pleases. It is not by looking to our personal interests or to political allegiances narrowly construed, that we should make up our mind. The citizen must decide on the basis of the principles of justice that underlie and guide the interpretation of the constitution and in the light of his sincere conviction as to how these principles should be applied in the circumstances. If he concludes that conditions obtain which justify civil disobedience and conducts himself accordingly, he has acted conscientiously and perhaps mistakenly, but not in any case at his convenience.

In a democratic society each man must act as he thinks the principles of political right require him to. We are to follow our understanding of these principles, and we cannot do otherwise. There can be no morally binding legal interpretation of these principles, not even by a supreme court or legislature. Nor is there any infallible procedure for determining what or who is right. In our system the Supreme Court, Congress, and the President often put forward rival interpretations of the Constitution. Although the Court has the final say in settling any particular case, it is not immune from powerful political influences that may change its reading of the law of the land. The Court presents its point of view by reason and argument; its conception of the Constitution must, if it is to endure, persuade men of its soundness. The final court of appeal is not the Court, or Congress, or the President, but the electorate as a whole. The civilly disobedient appeal in effect to this body. There is no danger of anarchy as long as there is a sufficient working agreement in men's conception of political justice and what it requires. That men can achieve such an understanding when the essential political liberties are maintained is the assumption implicit in democratic institutions. There is no way to avoid entirely the risk of divisive strife. But if legitimate civil disobedience seems to threaten civil peace, the responsibility falls not so much on those who protest as upon those whose abuse of authority and power justifies such opposition.

HERBERT MARCUSE

Ethics and Revolution

I propose to discuss the relation between ethics and revolution by taking as guidance the following question: Can a revolution be justified as right, as good, perhaps even as necessary, and justified not merely in political terms (as expedient for certain interests) but in ethical terms, that is to say, justified with respect to the human condition as such, to the potential of man in a given historical situation? This means that ethical terms such as "right" or "good" will be applied to political and social movements, with the hypothesis that the moral evaluation of such movements is (in a sense to be defined) more than subjective, more than a matter of preference. Under this hypothesis, "good" and "right" would mean serving to establish, to promote, or to extend human freedom and happiness in a commonwealth, regardless of the form of government. This preliminary definition combines individual and personal, private and public welfare. It tries to recapture a basic concept of classical political philosophy which has been all too often repressed, namely, that the end of government is not only the greatest possible freedom, but also the greatest possible happiness of man, that is to say, a life without fear and misery, and a life in peace.

Here we encounter the first vexing question, namely, who determines, who can and by what right determine the general interest of a commonwealth, and thereby determine the range and limits of individual freedom and happiness, and the sacrifices imposed upon individual freedom and happiness in the name and on behalf of the commonwealth? For as long as the general and individual welfare do not immediately coincide, the latter will be *made* to conform with the former. And if we ask this question we are at once confronted with an equally serious and embarrassing problem: granted even that freedom is not only an individual and private affair, that it is rather determined by the society, by the state in which we live, what about happiness? Is the happiness of an individual his own private affair, or is it too, in a very definite sense, subject to the limitations and even the definitions imposed upon it by a commonwealth? The extreme position that human happiness is and must remain individual and the individual's own affair cannot be defended if we give it only a few minutes' thought. There are certainly modes and types of individual happiness which cannot be tolerated by any kind of commonwealth. It is perfectly possible—as a matter of fact we know it to be the fact—that the people who were the master torturers in the Hitler concentration camps were often quite happy doing their job. This is one of the many cases of individual happiness where we do not hesitate to say that it is not merely the individual himself who can be and who can remain the judge of his own happiness. We assume a tribunal which is (actually or morally) entitled to "define" individual happiness.

Now after these preliminary clarifications, let me define what I mean by "revolution." by "revolution" I understand the overthrow of a legally established government and constitution by a social class or movement with the aim of altering the social as well as the political structure. This definition excludes all military coups, palace revolutions, and "preventive" counterrevolutions (such as Fascism and Nazism) because they do not alter the basic social structure. If we define revolution in this way we can move one step forward by saying that such a radical and qualitative change implies violence. Peaceful revolutions, if there are such things, if there can be such things, do not present any problem. We can therefore reformulate the initial question by asking: Is the revolutionary use of violence justifiable as a means for establishing or promoting human freedom and happiness? The question implies a very important assumption, namely, that there are rational criteria for determining the possibilities of human freedom and happiness available to a society in a specific historical situation. If there are no such rational criteria, it would be impossible to evaluate a political movement in terms of its chances to attain a greater extent or a higher degree of freedom and happiness in society.

But postulating the availability of rational standards and criteria for judging the given possibilities of human freedom and happiness means assuming that the ethical, moral standards are *historical* standards. If they are not, they remain meaningless abstractions. Applied to our question, this means that to claim an ethical and moral right, a revolutionary movement must be able to give rational grounds for its chances to grasp real possibilities of human freedom and happiness, and it must be able to demonstrate the adequacy of its means for obtaining this end. Only if the problem is placed in such a historical context, is it susceptible to rational discussion. Otherwise, only two positions remain open, namely, to reject *a priori* or to endorse *a priori* all revolution and revolutionary violence. Both positions, the affirmative as well as the negative one, offend against historical facts. It is, for example, meaningless to say that modern society *could* have come about without the English, American, and French Revolutions. It is also meaningless to say that all revolutionary violence had the same social function and consequences. The violence of the Civil Wars in seventeenth century England, the violence of the first French Revolution certainly had effects and consequences very different from those of the Bolshevik Revolution, and very different from the counterrevolutionary violence perpetrated by the Nazi and Fascist regimes. Moreover, the positions of *a priori* rejecting or *a priori* approving social and political violence would amount to sanctioning any change brought about in history, regardless of whether it would be in a progressive or regressive, liberating or enslaving direction.

A very brief glance at the historical development of our problem may facilitate the discussion. In classical political philosophy, revolutions were not considered as breaks of the historical continuum. Plato as well as Aristotle believed that revolutions were built into the very dynamic of politics, that they belonged to the historical and at the same time natural cycle of birth, growth and decay of political forms. In medieval and early modern philosophy the idea of a natural and divine order either outlawed all resistance to established government, or made resistance against tyranny not only a right but a moral duty and obligation. Then, in the sixteenth and seventeenth centuries, the practically unlimited right to resist a government, even to overthrow a government, was normally claimed by Protestant against Catholic, and by Catholic against Protestant regimes. A most characteristic reaction against these doctrines may be seen in the attitude towards revolution which we find in such different figures as Hobbes and Descartes, namely, that change is always to the worst. Leave the established social and political institutions as they are, for, no matter how bad they may be, the risk of overthrowing them is too great. Descartes, the great revolutionary in thought, was extremely conservative with respect to the "great public bodies." To them, doubt is not supposed to be extended, they are supposed to be left alone. At the same time, philosophers are strongly inclined to endorse a revolution once it has proved to be successful. Representative of this attitude is the case of Kant—certainly not a paragon of opportunism and expediency—who rejected the right of resistance and condemned revolt against established government, but added that, once a revolution has succeeded, a new legal government is established, and man owes obedience to the new revolutionary government just as he owed it to the government which was overthrown by the revolution.

On the other side of the fence, political theory and practice recognize historical situations in which violence becomes the necessary and essential element of progress. This concept is instrumental in the political theory and practice of totalitarian democracy. Robespierre calls for the "despotism of liberty" against the despotism of tyranny: in the fight for freedom, in the interest of the whole against the particular interests of oppression, terror may become a necessity and an obligation. Here, violence, revolutionary violence, appears not only as a political means but as a moral duty. The terror is defined as *counter*violence: it is "legitimate" only in defense against the oppressors and until they are defeated. Similarly, the Marxian concept of proletarian dictatorship is that of a transitional self-cancelling dictatorship: self-cancelling because it is supposed to last only as long as the power of the old ruling classes still combats the construction of the socialist society; after their defeat, the engines of repression were to be stopped. Here too, revolutionary violence is defined as counterviolence. The Marxian concept assumes that the old ruling classes would never voluntarily abdicate their position, that they would be the first to use violence against the revolution, and that revolutionary violence would be the defense against counterrevolutionary violence.

The theory of an educational, transitional dictatorship implies the paradoxical proposition that man must be "forced to be free." Political philosophy has always recognized the moral function of coercion (the coercive power of law, either above the sovereign or identical with the sovereign), but Rousseau provides a radically new justification. Coercion is necessitated by the immoral, repressive conditions under which men live. The basic idea is: how can slaves who do not even know they are slaves free themselves? How can they liberate themselves by their own power, by their own faculties? How can they spontaneously accomplish liberation? They must be taught and must be led to be free, and this the more so the more the society in which they live uses all available means in order to shape and preform their consciousness and to make it immune against possible alternatives. This idea of an educational, preparatory dictatorship has today become an integral element of revolution and of the justification of the revolutionary oppression. The dictatorships which began as revolutionary dictatorships and then perpetuated themselves claim to be in their very essence and structure transitional and preparatory for a stage at which they can be abolished by virtue of their own achievements.

The main argument against the notion of the transitional dictatorship is usually condensed in the question: who educates the educators? By what right do those who actually exercise the dictatorship speak in the name of freedom and happiness as general conditions? This argument by itself is not sufficient, because in a lesser degree it applies even to non-authoritarian societies, where the policy-making top layer is not constantly and effectively controlled from below. However, even if we concede that the majority of men are not yet free today, and that their liberation cannot be spontaneous, the question still remains whether the dictatorial means are adequate to attain the end, namely, liberation. In other words the question of a transitional dictatorship cannot be separated from the general question of whether there can be such a thing as a moral justification of suppression and violence in a revolution. I shall now briefly discuss this question.

The historical revolutions were usually advocated and started in the name of freedom, or rather in the name of greater freedom for more strata of the population. We must first examine this claim strictly on empirical grounds. Human freedom is not and never has been a static condition but an historical condition, a process which involves the radical alteration, and even negation, of established ways of life. The form and content of freedom change with every new stage in the development of civilization, which is man's increasing mastery of man and nature. In both modes, mastery means domination, control; more effective control of nature makes for more effective control of man. Obviously, the possibilities of human freedom and happiness in advanced industrial society today are in no way comparable with those available, even theoretically available, at preceding stages of history. Thus, with respect to the form, extent, degree and content of human freedom, we deal with strictly historical and changing conditions. We can say even more. Measured against the real possibilities of freedom, we always live in a state of relative unfreedom. The wide gap between real possibility and actuality, between the rational and the real has never been closed. Freedom always presupposes liberation, or a step from one state of freedom and unfreedom to a subsequent state. With the advance of technical progress, the later state is *potentially* (but by no means actually!) a *higher* stage, that is, quantitatively and qualitatively. But if this is the case, if freedom always presupposes liberation from unfree and unhappy conditions, it means that this liberation always offends against and ultimately subverts established and sanctioned institutions and interests. In history, they never abdicated voluntarily. Consequently, if and when freedom is a process of liberation, a transition from lower, more restricted forms of freedom to higher forms of freedom, then it always, no matter how, offends against the existing and established state of affairs. And precisely on this ground revolutionary violence has been most effectively justified as counterviolence, that is, as violence necessary in order to secure higher forms of freedom against the resistance of the established forms.

The ethics of revolution thus testifies to the clash and conflict of two historical rights: on the one side, the right of that which *is,* the established commonwealth on which the life and perhaps even the happiness of the individuals depend; and on the other side, the right of that which *can* be and perhaps even *ought* to be because it may reduce toil, misery, and injustice, provided always that this chance can be demonstrated as a real possibility. Such a demonstration must provide rational criteria; we can now add: these must be *historical* criteria. As such, they amount to an "historical calculus," namely, calculation of the chances of a future society as against the chances of the existing society with respect to human progress, that is to say, technical and material progress used in such a way that it increases individual freedom and happiness. Now if such an historical calculus is to have any rational basis, it must, on the one side, take into account the sacrifices exacted from the living generations on behalf of the established society, the established law and order, the number of victims made in defense of this society in war and peace, in the struggle for existence, individual and national. The calculus would further have to take into account the intellectual and material resources available to the society and the manner in which they are actually used with respect to their full capacity of satisfying vital human needs and pacifying the struggle for existence. On the other side, the historical calculus would have to project the chances of the contesting revolutionary movement of improving the prevailing conditions, namely, whether the revolutionary plan or program demonstrates the technical, material, and mental possibility of reducing the sacrifices and the number of victims. Even prior to the question as to the possibility of such a calculus (which, I believe, does exist), its inhuman quantifying character is evident. But its inhumanity is that of history itself, token of its empirical, rational foundation. No hypocrisy should from the beginning distort the examination. Nor is this brutal calculus an empty intellectual abstraction; in fact, at its decisive turns, history became such a calculated experiment.

The ethics of revolution, if there is such a thing, will therefore be in accordance not with absolute, but with historical standards. They do not cancel the validity of those general norms which formulate requirements for the progress of mankind toward humanity.

No matter how rationally one may justify revolutionary means in terms of the demonstrable chance of obtaining freedom and happiness for future generations, and thereby justify violating existing rights and liberties and life itself, there are forms of violence and suppression which no revolutionary situation can justify because they negate the very end for which the revolution is a means. Such are arbitrary violence, cruelty, and indiscriminate terror. However, within the historical continuum, revolutions establish a moral and ethical code of their own and in this way become the origin, the fountainhead and source of new general norms and values. In fact some of today's most generally-professed values originated in revolutions, for example, the value of tolerance in the English Civil Wars, the inalienable rights of man in the American and French Revolutions. These ideas become an historical force, first as partial ideas, instruments of a revolutionary movement for specific political ends. Their realization originally involved violence; they then assumed not only partial political but general ethical validity and rejected violence. In this way, revolutions place themselves under ethical standards.

Violence *per se* has never been made a revolutionary value by the leaders of the historical revolutions. His contemporaries rejected Georges Sorel's attempt to cut the link between violence and reason, which was at the same time the attempt to free the class struggle from all ethical considerations. In comparing the violence of the class struggle in its revolutionary phase with the violence of military operations in war, he made the former subject to strategic calculations only: the end was the total defeat of the enemy; violence a means to attain this end—the relation between means and end was a technical one. Sorel's defense of violence this side of good and evil remained isolated from the revolutionary reality of his time; if he had any influence, it was on the side of the counterrevolution. Otherwise, violence was defended, not *per se,* but as part of rational suppression, suppression of counterrevolutionary activity, of established rights and privileges, and, for the society at large, of material and intellectual needs, that is, enforcement of austerity, rationing, censorship.

Now this suppression which includes violence is practiced in the interest of the objectives of the revolution, and these objectives are presented not only as political but also as moral values, ethical imperatives, namely greater freedom for the greater number of people. And in this sense the objectives and the ends of the revolution itself claim general validity and become subject to moral standards and evaluation.

Here we are confronted with the problem of all ethics, namely, the question as to the ultimate sanction of moral values. Or, in plain language, who or what determines the validity of ethical norms? The question becomes acute only with the secularization of the West; it was no problem in the Middle Ages as long as a transcendent sanction of ethics was accepted. The infidels could justly be exterminated, heretics could justly be burned—in spite of all protest. This was justice in terms of the prevailing values, which in turn were those of transcendent ethics. But today, where is the sanction of ethical values—sanction not in terms of the enforcement but in terms of the acceptance of ethical values, the proof of their validity? Sanction today, it seems, rests mainly in a precarious and flexible syndrome of custom, fear, utility, and religion; flexible because, within the syndrome, there is a large range of change. I refer, for example, to the high degree of liberalization in sexual morality which we have witnessed during the last thirty years, or, to the easy suspension of practically all ethical values in so-called emergency situations. The sanction and validity of ethical norms is thus restricted to the normal state of affairs in social and political relations.

Now in terms of the normal established state of affairs, a revolution is by definition immoral; it offends against the right of the existing commonwealth; it permits and even demands deception, cunning, suppression, destruction of life and property, and so on. But a judgment by definition is an inadequate judgment. Ethical standards by virtue of their imperative claim transcend any given state of affairs, and they transcend it, not to any metaphysical entities but to the historical continuum in which every given state of affairs has emerged, by which every given state of affairs is defined, and in which every given state of affairs will be altered and surpassed by other states. And in the historical continuum which defines its place and function, the ethics of revolution appeal to an historical calculus. Can the intended new society, the society intended by the revolution, offer better chances for progress in freedom than the existing society? In the historical continuum, these chances can only be measured by going beyond the given state of affairs, going beyond it not simply into an abstract vacuum of speculation, but going beyond it by calculating the resources, intellectual as well as material, scientific as well as technical, available to a given society, and projecting the most rational ways of utilizing these resources. Now if such projection is possible, then it can yield objective criteria for judging revolutions as to their historical function in terms of progress or regression, in terms of the development of *humanitas*.

A preliminary answer is suggested by a glance at the historical process itself. Historically, the objective tendency of the great revolutions of the modern period was the enlargement of the social range of freedom and the enlargement of the satisfaction of needs. No matter how much the social interpretations of the English and French Revolutions may differ, they seem to agree in that a redistribution of the social wealth took place, so that previously less privileged or underprivileged classes were the beneficiaries of this change, economically and/or politically. In spite of subsequent periods of reaction and restoration, the result and objective function of these revolutions was the establishment of more liberal governments, a gradual democratization of society, and technical progress. I said "objective function" because this evaluation of the revolution is obviously a judgment *ex post facto*. The intention and ideology of the leaders of the revolution, and the drives of the masses may have had quite different aims and motives. By virtue of their objective function, these revolutions attained progress in the sense defined, namely, a demonstrable enlargement of the range of human freedom; they thus established, in spite of the terrible sacrifices exacted by them, an ethical right over and above all political justification.

But if such ethical right and its criteria are always and necessarily after the fact, it serves for nought and leaves us with the irrational choice of either *a priori* accepting or *a priori* rejecting all revolution. Now I submit that, while the historical function of a revolution becomes identifiable only after the fact, its prospective direction, progressive or regressive is, with the certainty of a rea-

sonable *chance,* demonstrable *before* the fact—to the same degree
to which the historical conditions of progress are demonstrable.
For example, it could be demonstrated—and it was demonstrated
before the fact—that the French Revolution of 1789 would give,
in terms of the historical calculus, a better chance for the development of human freedom than the Ancien Régime. Contrariwise, it
could be demonstrated, and was demonstrated long before the fact,
that Fascist and National-Socialist regimes would do the exact opposite, namely, necessarily restrict the range of human freedom.
Moreover, and I think this is a very important point, such demonstration of the historical *chances* before the fact becomes increasingly rational with the development of our scientific, technical, and
material resources and capabilities, with our progress in the scientific mastery of man and nature. The possibilities and contents of
freedom today are coming more and more under the control of
man: they are becoming increasingly calculable. And with this advance in effective control and calculability, the inhuman distinction
between violence and violence, sacrifice and sacrifice becomes increasingly rational. For throughout history, the happiness and freedom, and even the life of individuals, have been sacrificed. If we
consider human life *per se* sacred under all conditions, the distinction is meaningless, and we have to admit that history is *per se*
amoral and immoral, because it has never respected the sanctity of
human life as such. But in fact we do distinguish between sacrifices
which are legitimate and sacrifices which are not legitimate. This
distinction is an historical one, and with this qualification, ethical
standards are also applicable to violence.

Let me now recapitulate and reformulate. In absolute ethical
terms, that is to say, in terms of suprahistorical validity, there is
no justification for any suppression and sacrifice for the sake of
future freedom and happiness, revolutionary or otherwise. But in
historical terms we are confronted with a distinction and a decision.
For suppression and sacrifice are daily exacted by all societies, and
one cannot start—indeed I would like to say this with all possible
emphasis—one cannot start becoming moral and ethical at an arbitrary but expedient point of cut off: the point of revolution. Who
can quantify and who can compare the sacrifices exacted by an
established society and those exacted by its subversion? Are ten

thousand victims more ethical than twenty thousand? Such is in fact the inhuman arithmetic of history, and in this inhuman historical context operates the historical calculus. Calculable are the material and intellectual resources available, calculable are the productive and distributive facilities in a society, and the extent of unsatisfied vital needs and of satisfied nonvital needs. Quantifiable and calculable are the quantity and size of the labor force and of the population as a whole. That is the empirical material at the disposal of the historical calculus. And on the basis of this quantifiable material the question can be asked whether the available resources and capabilities are utilized most rationally, that is to say, with a view to the best possible satisfaction of needs under the priority of vital needs and with a minimum of toil, misery and injustice. If the analysis of a specific historical situation suggests a negative answer, if conditions exist in which technological rationality is impeded or even superseded by repressive political and social interests which define the general welfare, then the reversal of such conditions in favor of a more rational and human use of the available resources would also be a maximalization of the chance of progress in freedom. Consequently, a social and political movement in this direction would, in terms of the calculus, allow the presumption of historical justification. It can be no more than a presumption, subject to correction as the movement actually develops, reveals its potential and establishes new facts, or in other words, as it sustains or as it cuts the links between the means which the revolution employs and the end which it professes to attain.

And this leads to the last question which I want to raise here, namely, can the revolutionary end justify *all* means? Can we distinguish between rational and irrational, necessary and arbitrary, suppression? When can such suppression be called rational in terms of the objective of a respective revolution? I shall briefly illustrate the scope of this question by the Bolshevik Revolution. The professed objective of the Bolshevik Revolution was socialism. It implied the socialization of the means of production, the dictatorship of the proletariat as preparatory to a classless society. In the specific historical situation in which the Bolshevik Revolution occurred, socialism called for industrialization in competition with the advanced capitalist countries of the West, for the building up of the armed forces, and for propaganda on a global scale. Now can we apply a distinction between rational and irrational to these objectives and to the degree of suppression involved in them? In terms of the revolution, rational would be accelerated industrialization, the elimination of non-cooperative layers of management from the economy, the enforcement of work discipline, sacrifices in the satisfaction of needs imposed by the priority of heavy industry in the first stages of industrialization, and suspension of civil liberties if they were used for sabotaging these objectives. And we can reject, without long discussion, as not justifiable, even in terms of the revolution, the Moscow trials, the permanent terror, the concentration camps, and the dictatorship of the Party over the working classes. Further examination would require introducing into the discussion the situation of global coexistence; but time forbids us to do so. We have also made abstraction from the human element in the leadership of the revolution, that is to say, from the so-called historical individuals.

And here I want to add one remark. It seems to me characteristic that, the more calculable and the more controllable the technical apparatus of modern industrial society becomes, the more does the chance of human progress depend on the intellectual and moral qualities of the leaders, and on their willingness and ability to educate the controlled population and to make it recognize the possibility, nay, the necessity of pacification and humanization. For today, the technical apparatus of advanced industrial society is in itself authoritarian, requiring service, submission, subordination to the objective mechanism of the machine system, that is to say, submission to those who control the apparatus. Technology has been made into a powerful instrument of streamlined domination—the more powerful the more it proves its efficiency and delivers the goods. And as such, it serves the politics of domination.

I come to the conclusion. The means-end relation is the ethical problem of revolution. In one sense, the end justifies the means, namely, if they demonstrably serve human progress in freedom. This legitimate end, the only legitimate end, demands the creation of conditions which would facilitate and expedite its realization. And the creation of these conditions may justify sacrifices, as it has justified sacrifices throughout history. But this relation between means and ends is a dialectical one. The end must be operative in the repressive means for attaining the end. But no matter how rational, how necessary, how liberating—revolution involves violence. The non-violent history is the promise and possibility of a society which is still to be fought for. At present, the triumphant violence seems to be on the other side.

ROBERT PAUL WOLFF

On Violence

Everything I shall say in this essay has been said before, and much of it seems to me to be obvious as well as unoriginal. I offer two excuses for laying used goods before you. In the first place, I think that what I have to say about violence is true. Now, there are many ways to speak falsehood and only one way to speak truth. It follows, as Kierkegaard pointed out, that the truth is likely to become boring. On a subject as ancient and much discussed as ours today, we may probably assume that a novel—and, hence, interesting—view of violence is likely to be false.

But truth is not my sole excuse, for the subject before us suffers from the same difficulty that Kant discerned in the area of metaphysics. After refuting the various claims that had been made to transcendent rational knowledge of things-in-themselves, Kant remarked that the refutations had no lasting psychological effect on true believers. The human mind, he concluded, possessed a natural disposition to metaphysical speculation, which philosophy must perpetually keep in check. Somewhat analogously, men everywhere are prone to certain beliefs about the legitimacy of political authority, even though their beliefs are as groundless as metaphysical speculations. The most sophisticated of men persist in supposing that some valid distinction can be made between legitimate and illegitimate commands, on the basis of which they can draw a line, for example, between mere violence and the legitimate use of force. This lingering superstition is shared by those dissenters who call

"On Violence" by Robert Paul Wolff. From *Journal of Philosophy* 56, no. 19 (October 2, 1969): 601–16. Reprinted by permission of the author and the publisher.

police actions or ghetto living conditions "violent"; for they are merely advancing competing legitimacy claims.

I shall set forth and defend *three* propositions about violence:

First: The concept of violence is inherently confused, as is the correlative concept of nonviolence; these and related concepts depend for their meaning in political discussions on the fundamental notion of legitimate authority, which is also inherently incoherent.

Second: It follows that a number of familiar questions are also confusions to which no coherent answers could ever be given, such as: when it is permissible to resort to violence in politics; whether the black movement and the student movement should be nonviolent; and whether anything good in politics is ever accomplished by violence.

Finally: The dispute over violence and nonviolence in contemporary American politics is ideological rhetoric designed either to halt change and justify the existing distribution of power and privilege or to slow change and justify some features of the existing distribution of power and privilege or else to hasten change and justify a total redistribution of power and privilege.

Let us begin with the first proposition, which is essential to my entire discussion.

I

The fundamental concepts of political philosophy are the concepts of power and authority.[1] Power in general is the ability to make and enforce decisions. Political power is the ability to make and enforce decisions about matters of major social importance. Thus the ability to dispose of my private income as I choose is a

1. What follows is a summary of analyses I have published elsewhere. The concept of political power is treated in Chapter III of *The Poverty of Liberalism* (Boston: Beacon Press, 1968). The concepts of legitimacy and authority are analyzed in my essay on "Political Philosophy" in Arthur Danto, ed., *The Harper Guide to Philosophy* (New York: Harper & Row, 1970).

form of power, whereas the ability to make and enforce a decision about the disposition of some sizable portion of the tax receipts of the federal government is a form of *political* power. (So too is the ability to direct the decisions of a large private corporation; for the exercise of political power is not confined to the sphere of government.) A complete analysis of the concept of political power would involve a classification both of the means employed in the enforcing of decisions and of the scope and variety of questions about which decisions can be made.[2] It would also require an examination of the kinds of opposition against which the decision could be enforced. There is a very considerable difference between the ability a parliamentary majority has to enforce its decisions against the will of the minority and the ability of a rebel military clique to enforce its decisions against the Parliament as a whole.

Authority, by contrast with power, is not an ability but a right. It is the right to command and, correlatively, the right to be obeyed. Claims to authority are made in virtually every area of social life, and, in a remarkably high proportion of cases, the claims are accepted and acquiesced in by those over whom they are made. Parents claim the right to be obeyed by their children; husbands until quite recently claimed the right to be obeyed by their wives; popes claim the right to be obeyed by the laity and clergy; and of course, most notably, virtually all existing governments claim the right to be obeyed by their subjects.

A claim to authority must be sharply differentiated both from a threat or enticement and from a piece of advice. When the state commands, it usually threatens punishment for disobedience, and it may even on occasion offer a reward for compliance, but the command cannot be reduced to the mere threat or reward. What characteristically distinguishes a state from an occupying army or private party is its insistence, either explicit or implicit, on its *right* to be obeyed. By the same token, an authoritative command is not a mere recommendation. Authority says, "Do this!" not, "Let me suggest this for your consideration."

Claims to authority have been defended on a variety of grounds, most prominent among which are the appeal to God, to tradition,

2. See Robert A. Dahl, "The Concept of Power," *Behavioral Science* (July 1957), for just such a classification.

to expertise, to the laws of history, and to the consent of those commanded. We tend to forget that John Locke thought it worth while to devote the first of his *Two Treatises on Civil Government* to the claim that Europe's monarchs held their authority by right of primogenitural descent from Adam. It is common today to give lip service to the theory that authority derives from the consent of the governed, but most of us habitually accord *some* weight to any authority claim issuing from a group of men who regularly control the behavior of a population in a territory, particularly if the group tricks itself out with flags, uniforms, courts of law, and printed regulations.

Not all claims to authority are justified. Indeed, I shall suggest shortly that few if any are. Nevertheless, men regularly accept the authority claims asserted against them, and so we must distinguish a descriptive from a normative sense of the term. Let us use the term '*de facto* authority' to refer to *the ability to get one's authority claims accepted by those against whom they are asserted*. '*De jure* authority', then, will refer to *the right to command and to be obeyed*. Obviously, the concept of *de jure* authority is primary, and the concept of *de facto* authority is derivative.

Thus understood, *de facto* authority is a form of power, for it is a means by which its possessor can enforce his decisions. Indeed, as Max Weber—from whom much of this analysis is taken—has pointed out, *de facto* authority is the *principal* means on which states rely to carry out their decisions. Threats and inducements play an exceedingly important role in the enforcement of political decisions, to be sure, but a state that must depend upon them entirely will very soon suffer a crippling reduction in its effectiveness, which is to say, in its political power. Modern states especially require for the successful prosecution of their programs an extremely high level of coordination of the behavior of large numbers of individuals. The myth of legitimacy is the only efficient means available to the state for achieving that coordination.

Force is the ability to work some change in the world by the expenditure of physical effort. A man may root up a tree, move a stalled car, drive a nail, or restrain another man, *by force*. Force, in and of itself, is morally neutral. Physically speaking, there may be very little difference between the physical effort of a doctor who resets a dislocated shoulder and that of the ruffian who dislocated it. Sometimes, of course, force is used to work some change in the body of another man—to punch him, shoot him, take out his appendix, hold his arms, or cut his hair. But there is in principle no significant distinction between these uses of force and those uses which involve changing some other part of the world about which he cares. A man who slips into a parking place for which I am heading inflicts an injury on me roughly as great as if he had jostled me in a crowd or stepped on my toe. If he destroys a work of art on which I have lavished my most intense creative efforts, he may harm me more than a physical assault would.

Force is a means to power, but it is not of course a guarantee of power. If I wish to elicit hard work from my employees, I can threaten them with the lash or tempt them with bonuses—both of which are employments of force—but if my workers prefer not to comply, my threats and inducements may be fruitless. It is a commonplace both of domestic and of international politics that the mere possession of a monopoly of force is no guarantee of political power. Those who fail to grasp this truth are repeatedly frustrated by the baffling inability of the strong to impose their will upon the weak.

There are, so far as I can see, *three* means or instruments by which power is exercised—three ways, that is to say, in which men enforce or carry out their social decisions. The first is *force,* the ability to rearrange the world in ways that other men find appealing or distasteful. In modern society, money is of course the principal measure, exchange medium, and symbol of force. The second instrument of power is *de facto* authority—the ability to elicit obedience, as opposed to mere compliance, from others. *De facto* authority frequently accrues to those with a preponderance of force, for men are fatally prone to suppose that he who can compel compliance deserves obedience. But *de facto* authority does not reduce to the possession of a preponderance of force, for men habitually obey commands they know could not effectively be enforced. The third instrument of power is social opinion, or what might be called the "symbolic" use of force. When a runner competes in a race, he may want the first-prize money or the commercial endorsements that will come to the winner, or he may even just like blue ribbons—but he may also want the acclaim of the fans. Now, that acclaim is expressed by certain uses of force—by clapping of hands and cheering, which are physical acts. But its value to the runner is symbolic; he cherishes it as an expression of approval, not merely as a pleasing sound. To say that man is a social creature is not merely to say that he hangs out in groups, nor even to say that he engages in collective and co-operative enterprises for self-interested purposes; it is most importantly to say that he values symbolic interactions with other men and is influenced by them as well as by the ordinary exercise of force and by claims of authority. This point is important for our discussion, for, as we shall see, many persons who shrink from the use of force as an instrument of political power have no compunctions about the use of social opinion or what I have called the "symbolic" use of force. Anyone who has observed a progressive classroom run by a teacher with scruples of this sort will know that a day "in coventry" can be a far crueler punishment for an unruly ten-year old than a sharp rap on the knuckles with a ruler.

We come, finally, to the concept of violence. Strictly speaking, *violence is the illegitimate or unauthorized use of force to effect decisions against the will or desire of others.* Thus, murder is an act of violence, but capital punishment *by a legitimate state* is not; theft or extortion is violent, but the collection of taxes *by a legitimate state* is not. Clearly, on this interpretation the concept of violence is normative as well as descriptive, for it involves an implicit appeal to the principle of *de jure* legitimate authority. There is an associated sense of the term which is purely descriptive, relying on the descriptive notion of *de facto* authority. Violence in this latter sense is the use of force in ways that are proscribed or unauthorized by those who are generally accepted as the legitimate authorities in the territory. Descriptively speaking, the attack on Hitler's life during the second World War was an act of violence, but one might perfectly well deny that it was violent in the strict sense, on the grounds that Hitler's regime was illegitimate. On similar grounds, it is frequently said that police behavior toward workers or ghetto dwellers or demonstrators is violent even when it is clearly within the law, for the authority issuing the law is illegitimate.

It is common, but I think wrong-headed, to restrict the term 'violence' to uses of force that involve bodily interference or the direct infliction of physical injury. Carrying a dean out of his office is said to be violent, but not seizing his office when he is absent and locking him out. Physically tearing a man's wallet from his pocket is "violent," but swindling him out of the same amount of money is not. There is a natural enough basis for this distinction. Most of us value our lives and physical well-being above other goods that we enjoy, and we tend therefore to view attacks or threats on our person as different in kind from other sorts of harm we might suffer. Nevertheless, the distinction is not sufficiently sharp to be of any analytical use, and, as we shall see later, it usually serves the ideological purpose of ruling out, as immoral or politically illegitimate, the only instrument of power that is available to certain social classes.

In its strict or normative sense, then, the concept of political violence depends upon the concept of *de jure,* or legitimate authority. If there is no such thing as legitimate political authority, then it is impossible to distinguish between legitimate and illegitimate uses of force. Now, of course, under any circumstances, we can distinguish between right and wrong, justified and unjustified, uses of force. Such a distinction belongs to moral philosophy in general, and our choice of the criteria by which we draw the distinction will depend on our theory of value and obligation. But the distinctive political concept of violence can be given a coherent meaning *only* by appeal to a doctrine of legitimate political authority.

On the basis of a lengthy reflection upon the concept of *de jure* legitimate authority, I have come to the conclusion that philosophical anarchism is true. That is to say, I believe that there is not, and there could not be, a state that has a right to command and whose subjects have a binding obligation to obey. I have defended this view in detail elsewhere, and I can only indicate here the grounds of my conviction.[3] Briefly, I think it can be shown that every man has a fundamental duty to be autonomous, in Kant's sense of the term. Each of us must make himself the author of his actions and

3. See "Political Philosophy," in Danto, *op. cit.*

take responsibility for them by refusing to act save on the basis of reasons he can see for himself to be good. Autonomy, thus understood, is in direct opposition to obedience, which is submission to the will of another, irrespective of reasons. Following Kant's usage, political obedience is heteronymy of the will.

Now, political theory offers us one great argument designed to make the autonomy of the individual compatible with submission to the putative authority of the state. In a democracy, it is claimed, the citizen is both law-giver and law-obeyer. Since he shares in the authorship of the laws, he submits to his own will in obeying them, and hence is autonomous, not heteronymous.

If this argument were valid, it would provide a genuine ground for a distinction between violent and nonviolent political actions. Violence would be a use of force proscribed by the laws of executive authority of a genuinely democratic state. The only possible justification of illegal or extralegal political acts would be a demonstration of the illegitimacy of the state, and this in turn would involve showing that the commands of the state were not expressions of the will of the people.

But the classic defense of democracy is *not* valid. For a variety of reasons, neither majority rule nor any other method of making decisions in the absence of unanimity can be shown to preserve the autonomy of the individual citizens. In a democracy, as in any state, obedience is heteronymy. The autonomous man is of necessity an anarchist. Consequently, there is no valid *political* criterion for the justified use of force. Legality is, by itself, no justification. Now, of course, there are all manner of utilitarian arguments for submitting to the state and its agents, even if the state's claim to legitimacy is unfounded. The laws may command actions that are in fact morally obligatory or whose effects promise to be beneficial. Widespread submission to law may bring about a high level of order, regularity, and predictability in social relationships which is valuable independently of the particular character of the acts commanded. But in and of themselves, the acts of police and the commands of legislatures have no peculiar legitimacy or sanction. Men everywhere and always impute authority to established governments, and they are always wrong to do so.

II

The foregoing remarks are quite banal, to be sure. Very few serious students of politics will maintain either the democratic theory of legitimate authority or any alternatives to it. Nevertheless, like post-theological, demythologized Protestants who persist in raising prayers to a God they no longer believe in, modern men go on exhibiting a superstitious belief in the authority of the state. Consider, for example, a question now much debated: When is it permissible to resort to violence in politics? If "violence" is taken to mean an *unjustified* use of force, then the answer to the question is obviously *never*. If the use of force were permissible, it would not, by definition, be violence, and if it were violent, it would not, by definition, be permissible. If 'violence' is taken in the strict sense to mean "an illegitimate or unauthorized use of force," then *every* political act, whether by private parties or by agents of the state, is violent, for there is no such thing as legitimate authority. If 'violence' is construed in the restricted sense as "bodily interference or the direct infliction of physical harm," then the obvious but correct rule is to resort to violence when less harmful or costly means fail, providing always that the balance of good and evil produced is superior to that promised by any available alternative.

These answers are all trivial, but that is precisely my point. Once the concept of violence is seen to rest on the unfounded distinction between legitimate and illegitimate political authority, the question of the appropriateness of violence simply dissolves. It is mere superstition to describe a policeman's beating of a helpless suspect as "an excessive use of force" while characterizing an attack by a crowd on the policeman as "a resort to violence." The implication of such a distinction is that the policeman, as the duly appointed representative of a legitimate government, has a right to use physical force, although no right to use "excessive" force, whereas the crowd of private citizens has no right at all to use even moderate physical force. But there are no legitimate governments, hence no special rights attaching to soldiers, policemen, magistrates, or other law-enforcement agents, hence no coherent distinction between violence and the legitimate use of force.

Consider, as a particular example, the occupation of buildings and the student strike at Columbia University during April and May of 1968. The consequences of those acts have not yet played themselves out, but I think certain general conclusions can be drawn. First, the total harm done by the students and their supporters was very small in comparison with the good results that were achieved. A month of classwork was lost, along with many tempers and a good deal of sleep. Someone—it is still not clear who —burned the research notes of a history professor, an act which, I am happy to say, produced a universal revulsion shared even by the SDS. In the following year, a number of classes were momentarily disrupted by SDS activists in an unsuccessful attempt to repeat the triumph of the previous spring.

Against this, what benefits flowed from the protest? A reactionary and thoroughly unresponsive administration was forced to resign; an all-university Senate of students, professors, and administrators was created, the first such body at Columbia. A callous and antisocial policy of university expansion into the surrounding neighborhood was reversed; some at least of the university's ties with the military were loosened or severed; and an entire community of students and professors were forced to confront moral and political issues which till then they had managed to ignore.

Could these benefits have been won at less cost? Considering the small cost of the uprising, the question seems to me a bit finicky; nevertheless, the answer is clearly, No. The history of administrative intransigence and faculty apathy at Columbia makes it quite clear that nothing short of a dramatic act such as the seizure of buildings could have deposed the university administration and produced a university senate. In retrospect, the affair seems to have been a quite prudent and restrained use of force.

Assuming this assessment to be correct, it is tempting to conclude, "In the Columbia case, violence was justified." But this conclusion is *totally wrong*, for it implies that a line can be drawn between legitimate and illegitimate forms of protest, the latter being justified only under special conditions and when all else has failed. We would all agree, I think, that, under a dictatorship, men have the right to defy the state or even to attack its representatives when their interests are denied and their needs ignored—the only rule

that binds them is the general caution against doing more harm
than they accomplish good. My purpose here is simply to argue
that a modern industrial democracy, whatever merits it may have,
is in this regard no different from a dictatorship. No special authority attaches to the laws of a representative, majoritarian state; it is
only superstition and the myth of legitimacy that invests the judge,
the policeman, or the official with an exclusive right to the exercise
of certain kinds of force.

In the light of these arguments, it should be obvious that I see no
merit in the doctrine of nonviolence, nor do I believe that any special and complex justification is needed for what is usually called
"civil disobedience." A commitment to nonviolence can be understood in two different senses, depending on the interpretation given
to the concept of violence. If violence is understood in the strict
sense as the political use of force in ways proscribed by a legitimate
government, then of course the doctrine of nonviolence depends
upon the assumption that there *are* or *could be* legitimate governments. Since I believe this assumption to be false, I can attribute no
coherent meaning to this first conception of nonviolence.

If violence is understood, on the other hand, as the use of force
to interfere with someone in a direct, bodily way or to injure him
physically, then the doctrine of nonviolence is merely a subjective
queasiness having no moral rationale. When you occupy the seats
at a lunch counter for hours on end, thereby depriving the pro-
prietor of the profits he would have made on ordinary sales during
that time, you are taking money out of his pocket quite as effectively as if you had robbed his till or smashed his stock. If you persist in the sit-in until he goes into debt, loses his lunch counter, and
takes a job as a day laborer, then you have done him a much greater
injury than would be accomplished by a mere beating in a dark
alley. He may deserve to be ruined, of course, but, if so, then he
probably also deserves to be beaten. A penchant for such indirect
coercion as a boycott or a sit-in is morally questionable, for it
merely leaves the dirty work to the bank that forecloses on the
mortgage or the policeman who carries out the eviction. Emotion-
ally, the commitment to nonviolence is frequently a severely repressed expression of extreme hostility akin to the mortifications
and self-flagellations of religious fanatics. Enough testimony has

come from Black novelists and psychiatrists to make it clear that
the philosophy of nonviolence is, for the American Negro, what
Nietzsche called a "slave morality"—the principal difference is that,
in traditional Christianity, God bears the guilt for inflicting pain
on the wicked; in the social gospel, the law acts as the scourge.

The doctrine of civil disobedience is an American peculiarity
growing out of the conflict between the authority claims of the state
and the directly contradictory claims of individual conscience. In a
futile attempt to deny and affirm the authority of the state simultaneously, a number of conscientious dissenters have claimed the
right to disobey what they believe to be immoral laws, so long as
they are prepared to submit to punishment by the state. A willingness to go to jail for one's beliefs is widely viewed in this country as
evidence of moral sincerity, and even as a sort of argument for the
position one is defending.

Now, tactically speaking, there is much to be said for legal mar-
tyrdom. As tyrannical governments are perpetually discovering, the
sight of one's leader nailed to a cross has a marvelously bracing effect on the faithful members of a dissident sect. When the rulers
are afflicted by the very principles they are violating, even the
threat of self-sacrifice may force a government to its knees. But
leaving tactics aside, no one has any moral obligation whatsoever
to resist an unjust government openly rather than clandestinely.
Nor has anyone a duty to invite and then to suffer unjust punishment. The choice is simple: if the law is right, follow it. If the law
is wrong, evade it.

I think it is possible to understand why conscientious and morally concerned men should feel a compulsion to seek punishment
for acts they genuinely believe to be right. Conscience is the echo
of society's voice within us. The men of strongest and most independent conscience are, in a manner of speaking, just those who
have most completely internalized this social voice, so that they
hear and obey its commands even when no policeman compels their
compliance. Ironically, it is these same men who are most likely to
set themselves against the government in the name of ideals and
principles to which they feel a higher loyalty. When a society violates the very principles it claims to hold, these men of conscience
experience a terrible conflict. They are deeply committed to the

principles society has taught them, principles they have truly come to believe. But they can be true to their beliefs only by setting themselves against the laws of the very society that has been their teacher and with whose authority they identify themselves. Such a conflict never occurs in men of weak conscience, who merely obey the law, however much it violates the moral precepts they have only imperfectly learned.

The pain of the conflict is too great to be borne; somehow, it must be alleviated. If the commitment to principle is weak, the individual submits, though he feels morally unclean for doing so. If the identification with society is weak, he rejects the society and becomes alienated, perhaps identifying with some other society. But if both conscience and identification are too strong to be broken, the only solution is to expiate the guilt by seeking social punishment for the breach of society's laws. Oddly enough, the expiation, instead of bringing them back into the fold of law-obeyers, makes it psychologically all the easier for them to continue their defiance of the state.

III

The foregoing conclusions seem to reach far beyond what the argument warrants. The classical theory of political authority may indeed be inadequate; it may even be that the concept of legitimate authority is incoherent; but surely *some* genuine distinction can be drawn between a politics of reason, rules, and compromise on the one hand, and the resort to violent conflict on the other! Are the acts of a rioting mob different only in degree from the calm and orderly processes of a duly constituted court of law? Such a view partakes more of novelty than of truth!

Unless I very much misjudge my audience, most readers will respond roughly in this manner. There may be a few still willing to break a lance for sovereignty and legitimate authority, and a few, I hope, who agree immediately with what I have said, but the distinction between violence and nonviolence in politics is too familiar to be so easily discarded. In this third section of my essay, therefore, I shall try to discover what makes the distinction so plausible, even though it is—I insist—unfounded.

The customary distinction between violent and nonviolent modes of social interaction seems to me to rest on *two* genuine distinctions: the first is the *subjective* distinction between the regular or accepted and the irregular or unexpected uses of force; the second is the *objective* distinction between those interests which are central or vital to an individual and those which are secondary or peripheral.

Consider first the subjective distinction between regular and irregular uses of force in social interactions. It seems perfectly appropriate to us that a conflict between two men who desire the same piece of land should be settled in favor of the one who can pull more money out of his pocket. We consider it regular and orderly that the full weight of the police power of the state be placed behind that settlement in order to ensure that nothing upset it. On the other hand, we consider it violent and disorderly to resolve the dispute by a fist fight or a duel. Yet what is the difference between the use of money, which is one kind of force, and the use of fists, which is another? Well, if we do not appeal to the supposed legitimacy of financial transactions or to the putative authority of the law, then the principal difference is that we are accustomed to settling disputes with dollars and we are no longer accustomed to settling them with fists.

Imagine how barbaric, how unjust, how *violent*, it must seem, to someone unfamiliar with the beauties of capitalism, that a man's ability to obtain medical care for his children should depend solely on the contingency that some other man can make a profit from his productive labor! Is the Federal Government's seizure of my resources for the purpose of killing Asian peasants less violent than a bandit's extortion of tribute at gunpoint? Yet we are accustomed to the one and unaccustomed to the other.

The objective distinction between central and peripheral interests also shapes our conception of what is violent in politics. When my peripheral or secondary interests are at stake in a conflict, I quite naturally consider only a moderate use of force to be justified. Anything more, I will probably call "violence." What I tend to forget, of course, is that other parties to the conflict may find their primary interests challenged and, hence, may have a very different view of what is and is not violent. In the universities, for example, most of the student challenges have touched only on the peripheral interests of professors. No matter what is decided about ROTC, curriculum, the disposition of the endowment, or Black studies, the typical philosophy professor's life will be largely unchanged. His tenure, salary, working conditions, status, and family life remain the same. Hence he is likely to take a tolerant view of building seizures and sit-ins. But let a classroom be disrupted, and he cries out that violence has no place on campus. What he means is that force has been used in a way that touches one of his deeper concerns.

The concept of violence serves as a rhetorical device for proscribing those political uses of force which one considers inimical to one's central interests. Since different social groups have different central interests and can draw on different kinds of force, it follows that there are conflicting definitions of violence. Broadly speaking, in the United States today, there are four conceptions of violence corresponding to four distinct socioeconomic classes.

The first view is associated with the established financial and political interests in the country. It identifies the violent with the illegal, and condemns all challenges to the authority of the state and all assaults on the rights of property as beyond the limits of permissible politics. The older segments of the business community adopt this view, along with the military establishment and the local elites of middle America. Robert Taft was once a perfect symbol of this sector of opinion.

The second view is associated with the affluent, educated, technical and professional middle class in America, together with the new, rapidly growing, future-oriented sectors of the economy, such as the communications industry, electronics, etc. They accept, even welcome, dissent, demonstration, ferment, and—within limits—attacks on property in ghetto areas. They look with favor on civil disobedience and feel at ease with extralegal tactics of social change. Their interests are identified with what is new in American society, and they are confident of coming out on top in the competition for wealth and status within an economy built on the principle of reward for profitable performance.

The "liberals," as this group is normally called, can afford to encourage modes of dissent or disruption that do not challenge the economic and social arrangements on which their success is based. They will defend rent strikes, grape boycotts, or lunch-counter sit-ins with the argument that unemployment and starvation are a form of violence also. Since they are themselves in competition with the older elite for power and prestige, they tend to view student rebels and black militants as their allies, up to the point at which their own interests are attacked. But when tactics are used that threaten their positions in universities, in corporations, or in affluent suburbs, then the liberals cry *violence* also, and call for the police. A poignant example of this class is the liberal professor who cheers the student rebels as they seize the Administration building and then recoils in horror at the demand that he share his authority to determine curriculum and decide promotions.

The third view of violence is that held by working-class and lower-middle-class Americans, those most often referred to as the "white backlash." They perceive the principal threat to their interests as coming from the bottom class of ghetto dwellers, welfare clients, and nonunionized laborers who demand more living space, admission to union jobs with union wages, and a larger share of the social product. To this hard-pressed segment of American society, "violence" means street crime, ghetto riots, civil-rights marches into all-white neighborhoods, and antiwar attacks on the patriotic symbols of constituted authority with which backlash America identifies. Studies of the petty bourgeoisie in Weimar Germany suggest, and George Wallace's presidential campaign of 1968 confirms, that the lower middle class, when it finds itself pressed between inflationary prices and demands from the lower class, identifies its principal enemy as the lower class. So we find the classic political alliance of old established wealth with right-wing populist elements, both of which favor a repressive response to attacks on authority and a strong governmental policy toward the "violence" of demands for change.

The fourth view of violence is the revolutionary counterdefinition put forward by the outclass and its sympathizers within the liberal wing of the established order. Two complementary rhetorical devices are employed. First, the connotation of the term "violence" is accepted, but the application of the term is reversed: police are violent, not rioters; employers, not strikers; the American army, not the enemy. In this way, an attack is mounted on the government's claim to possess the right to rule. Secondly, the denotation of the term is held constant and the connotation reversed. Violence is good, not bad; legitimate, not illegitimate. It is, in H. Rapp Brown's great rhetorical flourish, "as American as cherry pie." Since the outclass of rebels has scant access to the instruments of power used by established social classes—wealth, law, police power, legislation —it naturally seeks to legitimize the riots, harassments, and street crime which are its only weapons. Equally naturally, the rest of society labels such means "violent" and suppresses them.

In the complex class struggle for wealth and power in America, each of us must decide for himself which group he will identify with. It is not my purpose here to urge one choice rather than another. My sole aim is to argue that the concept of violence has no useful role to play in the deliberations leading to that choice. Whatever other considerations of utility and social justice one appeals to, no weight should be given to the view that *some* uses of force are prima facie ruled out as illegitimate and hence "violent" or that other uses of force are prima facie ruled in as legitimate, or legal. Furthermore, in the advancement of dissenting positions by illegal means, no special moral merit attaches to the avoiding, as it were, of body contact. Physical harm may be among the most serious injuries that can be done to an opponent, but, if so, it differs only in degree and not in kind from the injuries inflicted by so-called "nonviolent" techniques of political action.

IV

The myth of legitimate authority is the secular reincarnation of that religious superstition which has finally ceased to play a significant role in the affairs of men. Like Christianity, the worship of the state has its fundamentalists, its revisionists, its ecumenicists (or world-Federalists), and its theological rationale. The philosophical anarchist is the atheist of politics. I began my discussion with the observation that the belief in legitimacy, like the penchant for transcendent metaphysics, is an ineradicable irrationality of the human experience. However, the slow extinction of religious faith over the past two centuries may encourage us to hope that in time anarchism, like atheism, will become the accepted conviction of enlightened and rational men.

GIDON GOTTLIEB

Is Law Dead?

I

The crisis of law in America today has reached alarming dimensions. It was symbolically expressed earlier this year in the centennial celebrations of the Association of the Bar of the City of New York, a venerable and staid establishment institution. "Is law dead?" was the theme of their anniversary proceedings. This crisis of law has been sharpened by a convergence of civil disobedience, riots, violence, the black revolution, and government lawlessness. Antiquated theories and expectations, unable to cope with the emergence of the postindustrial world, have contributed to the impression that our legal order is in an advanced state of decay. A study of this decay should begin with a realistic assessment of civil disobedience.

The most salient feature of recent forms of civil disobedience is its communal or group-character. This is the feature that most requires emphasis for an understanding of the rejection of law by important elements in our society. Traditionally, civil disobedience has been analyzed in the context of the relationship between the state and the individual. The individual's conscience was characteristically described as pitted against the power of the state, as when Socrates and Thoreau invoked their personal convictions in matters of great public moment.

But civil disobedience is now a societal and political phenomenon much more than an individual, moral problem. It is an indicator of the disaffection of whole segments of our society, evidence of the rejection of the authority of the state. The issue was, therefore, correctly perceived in terms of legitimacy, the acceptance of authority, and what has been called the survival of a "society of consent" —namely, a society in which "the powers of government are just . . . that is, they are legitimate, because authorized and renewed by procedures of voting all must respect." And it is indeed the withdrawal of acceptance by powerful groups that now threatens faith in law.

At this point, however, a major source of confusion must be avoided: the withdrawal of acceptance of state authority is not tantamount to an assertion of the right to revolution. The withdrawal of acceptance may only be a strategic device for a restoration of legitimate rule by vigorous dissent, protest, resistance, or even rebellion. Admittedly, however, it may also pave the way for a complete takeover and transformation of state authority-structures fully deserving the name of revolution. Not all group resistance is, therefore, revolutionary—quite the contrary. Some such resistance may be designed to realize the full promise of accepted constitutional texts and political pledges. All group resistance does, however, stimulate confrontation, social tensions, and backlashes, and raises the threat of reaction and repression. Violent dissent, uprisings, and limited, sporadic civil strife are evil genies that are hard to control once released from the body politic, but they should not be confused with the specter of revolution. Indeed, it is by no means clear that revolution is at all possible in an advanced society such as ours. What has been called the advent of the "technetronic age" could well render revolutions obsolete. Securing physical control of power-centers such as communications facilities and networks is a manageable task in many countries—as colonels thinking of military *coups* know well. But in our highly-computerized society, with its intricate technology and diffusion of power-centers, not much can be achieved by raw power alone, save, that is, for the paralysis and terrorization of the population. The dictates of long-term corporate planning, capital management, orderly administration, demand-control, and technocratic manpower have been vividly and provocatively portrayed in Galbraith's *New Industrial State* and in Marcuse's *One-Dimensional Man*. If the delicate apparatus of modern power, the communication- and informa-tion-system, is a helpless hostage to violent dissent, it should prove, nevertheless, unmanageable in the hands of a revolutionary clique of any kind. Unless, that is, the full weight of modern surveillance and repressive technology is brought to bear by a ruthless, bureau-cratic, and technological elite, in a fully totalitarian regime along the lines of Orwell's *1984*—the feasibility of which we still merci-fully ignore.

Having thus summarily disposed of the specter of revolution, I would like to return to the question of civil disobedience, or what should be more aptly called "group disobedience" or "group re-sistance." The groups challenging the state's authority in our society are characterized by their ability to inflict severe civil disorder, to "tear society apart," and bring it to a near standstill. Black militants, student radicals, white supremacists, rebellious labor unions, mili-tant police forces, national guards, and other extremist groups all have the power to bring the nation to the edge of civil strife if not beyond. None of them, either singly or in combination, could conceivably operate the vast and intricate administrative-techne-tronic machinery of the modern industrial state. Yet all of them have acquired in a sense a *"veto" over the status quo,* a power to bring business-as-usual to a stop, a power to make other groups painfully aware of a *status quo* they reject. This is a very real kind of power, for it does endow these groups with a measure of capa-bility to gain their ends over the opposition of other centers of power, even, at times, over the opposition of a disorganized majority.

To put the matter differently, the business of the nation cannot be conducted harmoniously without a measure of consensus em-bracing these *"veto-communities."* This sets a serious limitation on the effectiveness of majority-rule and one that should be borne carefully in mind by designers of a Southern strategy or of any other strategy consciously intended to neglect a relevant community of the nation. It is a limitation bound to gain significance as ad-ministrations seek to legitimize policies in opinion-polls that do not reflect the vehemence of veto-community attitudes. It is a limitation that new technology will make even more significant. The possible onset of direct, computerized television audience-polling on national or local issues requires that limitations on the workability of majority rule be restudied and that the pitfalls of government by referendum be kept clearly in mind.

It should be fairly plain that veto-communities cannot be effectively repressed by the state without a substantial transformation in our system of government. The first chilling symptoms of such modification are already manifest. Effective repression would require a measure of suspension of our cherished civil liberties, invasions of privacy with the help of electronic spying devices, police surveillance of dissenters, centralized and computerized data banks of information on every citizen, preventive detention of agitators, control of the media (especially of television and its news coverage), the intimidation of universities, and financial pressures on educational and research foundations engaged in social and political concerns, as well as occasional blood-baths to discourage public confrontations.

Effective repression, in other words, would take us down the road toward a dreaded fully-administered bureaucratic-technological-authoritarian state in which not only probing investigations and unorthodox ideas but also deviant life-styles would be heavily penalized. The veto-communities of the nation wield power, therefore, not only on the *status quo* but also on the quality and character of our system of government. They have become in the process important instruments for change and not always for the good. Ironically, not even the reactionary veto-communities can protect the *status quo*. The very resort to violent clashes, brutality, and reprisals, to which some police and labor elements are increasingly prone, merely fans the fires of civil disorder and the anguish of the majority. They, no less than the advocates of change, thus pave the way either to social change or to repressive rule but in no case to the maintenance of the *status quo*.

Government dependent on a tacit concert of veto-communities is an ugly prospect for our political future. It suggests that our domestic order increasingly resembles the unquiet and threatening world of international relations. These semi-autonomous communities, autonomous that is in a sociological and not in a legal sense, now reject majority rule in the country. Their expectations and demands are legitimated in their own groups' perceptions—not in community acceptance of their demands. They are prepared to hold the nation to ransom to achieve their objectives. Already, in the wake of the Newark riots in 1967, the mayor of that city sought to restore peace by obtaining the collaboration of his city's veto-communities, the white militants, the black militants and the police. With the spread of veto-communities on a national and local level, realistic strategies, taking this phenomenon into account, must be designed for securing compliance with the law. Student disruptions on campuses have thus led some university administrators to adopt a delicate balance between policies of conciliation and enforcement. University presidents, not unlike United Nations diplomats, are frequently divided between resort to "Chapter VI" procedures for peaceful settlement or to "Chapter VII" procedures for enforcement-actions. Indeed, the similarities between key stages in the crisis at Columbia and, for example, the 1956 crisis in the Middle East are not fortuitous. In both places, accommodation and enforcement-strategies were tried and peace-making forces established. In both places the conflict involved large and powerful groups.

Spreading doubts about the feasibility of law enforcement against veto-communities are leading to second thoughts about coercive peace-enforcement strategies, both domestically and internationally. Accommodation between hostile communities and the maintenance of some form of peaceful co-existence appear increasingly attractive as against the exorbitant societal and political costs of strict law-enforcement.

II

The trouble with our legal order is that it is utterly unprepared to respond to the political and societal developments that have already taken place. Expectations about law and order, about the enforcement of laws, about punishment, about hierarchical authority-structures, about the state as the alleged repository of a monopoly of power, about the expression of consent through elections, about the illegitimacy of resistance to validly-elected authorities, about the shared values or "concordia" of society—all these expectations are being challenged. All require reassessment in light of group resistance and the widening distribution of power between com-

munities and groups within the state. For what has happened is
not only the actual erosion of the state's monopoly of power, but
also the widespread realization that this loss of power has taken
place. Nothing has done more than television to bring home the
horrors and uselessness of violence and repression. From Kesanh,
to Chicago, to Kent, to Berkeley, and to Jackson, the failure of
coercion was made apparent to millions of viewers. Unchecked riots
were followed by unchecked illegal labor strikes. Sanitation men,
transportation workers, policemen, teachers, firemen, and postal
workers all joined the parade of law-breakers. They were all put in
that position by unenforceable legislation prohibiting strikes of public employees, legislation that did not provide effective procedures to
meet labor claims. The disappointment of expectations resulting
from unenforced laws spread even more in the wake of the black
riots, during which the police stood by while businesses were
looted and property destroyed. The belief accordingly grew that
the law did not matter as much as those who occupied the seats of
power. This belief may have had something to do with the rise of
confrontations aimed at the "power structure," with the pitting of
power against power, of black power against white racism, and of
student power against police power. Law and its enforcement became a paper-tiger. Staggering crime statistics, corruption among
the police and in local governments, corporate frauds, the immu-
nity of organized crime, the mounting evidence of lawlessness at
all levels of society, massive drug-addiction problems—all these
merely compound the evident failure of coercive action rendered so
dramatic in confrontations with the veto-communities.

These phenomena can perhaps be given some degree of ordered
expression on the more arid plane of analytic discourse. Governing
elites, the legal profession, and the "man on the Queens subway"
share a fairly uniform implicit theory of law. That theory of law
received its classical exposition in the writings of John Austin in
the nineteenth century. It was strongly anchored in a Hobbesian
view, in a hierarchical conception of the state, in the relationship
between a political sovereign and political subordinates, in a relationship of authority and obedience. The pyramidal concept of
state-power made it possible to ground the law in the capability to
inflict sanctions. The close conceptual ties between law and sanc-

tions is still the basis of the implicit theory of law of our society. For law without penalty, law without credible sanctions—international law, for example—is still taken lightly by a legal profession reluctant to revise inherited modes of thought and expectations.

The emergence in this century of new centers of power in a position to compete with the power of the state itself has radically altered the political realities in which the vertical, pyramidal, sanction-oriented concept of law originally evolved. But the stubborn refusal to alter conceptual expectations in the face of contrary social trends continues. It received perhaps its purest expression in Kelsen's *Principles of International Law,* in which he postulated a monopoly of coercive forces in an imaginary world-order in which international enforcement-actions would sanction breaches of international law. Though the necessary connections between a legal system and its societal context are now gaining increasing recognition, legal theory is still largely dominated by the nation-state model allegedly endowed with a monopoly of coercive power. In international law studies, however, concern with legal arrangements in horizontal or nonhierarchical systems between fairly equal centers of power has led to the growth of new theories; but these studies have as yet scarcely penetrated the mainstream of juridical consciousness.

In speaking of the "death of law" we should make the identity of the patient no less clear than the fatal diagnosis itself. What is dying, I would submit, is a concept of law appropriate for a bygone society, for a hierarchically-organized society, relying upon the state's omnipotence against isolated, relatively helpless individuals. What is dying is a set of expectations accompanying the simple vision of law as superior power. What is dying is the pretense of enforcement in the face of an unbridgeable credibility gap; what is also dying is the faith that democracy can rely on the consent of individuals alone, paying no heed to the acceptance of authority by distinct community groups.

Much of what is now perceived as the pathology of a decaying legal order may soon be perceived as the emergence of a new concept of law. This new concept would set realistic expectations for an increasingly egalitarian system of power relationships between semiautonomous communities and the state. Such a system may look to accommodation rather than to sanctions in group conflicts; it may look to a consensus about accepted principles and policies, accepted, that is, by all relevant communities including the veto-communities. It may look to mediation, collective bargaining, negotiations, and to new imaginative settlement-procedures. An *acceptance-oriented concept of law* may gradually displace the now unworkable sanction-oriented model, at least insofar as veto-communities are concerned. The traditional, hierarchical concept of law, freed of its burden of failure, may then operate more effectively in the sphere that is properly its own—where the society and the individual—not groups—are involved. Admittedly, the emergence of a new concept of law might raise formidable new problems on a practical as well as on an analytic plane. Yet the shape of the new concept is already discernible in the horizontalist legal theories. The erosion of monolithic national authority-structures, the proliferation of domestic power-centers, of multinational corporations and agencies are all factors contributing to the cracking of outworn expectations.

Confusion about the nature of the legal order tragically obscures the urgent need for new institutional arrangements. Peaceful settlement-techniques in collective strife-situations are now exposed to the hazards of local politics and prejudices. Conflict-control mechanisms are almost entirely lacking—use of the police and of the guards in civil disorders constitute in themselves a source of such disorders. The absence of peace-keeping—as distinct from law-enforcement—instruments for conflict-control has left the field open for the escalation of violence. The two functions of law-enforcement and peace-keeping cannot be performed by the same instruments.

New legal arrangements are also needed where the poor, the blacks, and ethnic minorities are concerned. Effective grievance-machinery for terminating the malignant neglect of millions of American poor has yet to be established. Legal doctrines recognizing the group-consciousness and the group-rights of American blacks are yet to be articulated. The development of "class-actions" has not successfully met the acute needs for the juridical organization of students, the poor, slum dwellers, consumers, and other dissatisfied segments of the society. Indeed, problem-clusters relating to veto-communities still go largely without legal recognition. The connections between racism, poverty, unemployment, urban decay, crime, and alienation still defy comprehensive *juridical* analysis. In vital respects, group-rights lack effective legal vehicles for their defense. The law of unincorporated associations, labor law, certification and representation problems, and class-actions have all been resorted to in pressing for such rights. The law's coolness to these rights, its resistance to the growth of powerful organizations largely immune to state pressure, has been overcome in the past to permit the development of labor unions, and vast corporations and conglomerates. Churches, foundations, and universities, together with business and labor, secured juridical forms for their activities. The question is whether the same will now be true for some of the veto-communities in our country.

III

No discussion of the "death of law" would be complete without reference to the black community. Viewed from their perspective, the death of law is a misnomer. As far as they can see, it has never lived enough to die—it was stillborn. The promise of our most cherished legal and constitutional instruments was at no time fulfilled for the vast majority of black citizens. The apparatus of law appears to them as an oppressive enforcement-system designed to protect neighboring white communities while abandoning black communities to local violence and lawlessness. Remedial legislation in the areas of rent, rehabilitation, health, grants, and welfare was in large measure defeated by profiteering bureaucracies and corrupt inspection and enforcement personnel. Despite the selfless devotion and courage of civil-rights advocates, the attempt to bring the black population of the nation *as individuals* into the community of consent failed for the majority. The path outlined by the Fourteenth Amendment and followed with determination by the Warren Court was to provide an *individual* solution for black citizens as American citizens and to protect their rights to the equal protection of the laws. The civil-rights decisions and the attempted removal of racial barriers was one of the noblest efforts in twentieth-century American history, but it still left the situation of the black community as a whole relatively intolerable. It certainly failed to bring black Americans into the community of consent from which they had been excluded when the federation was established. Neither the black population nor the Indian nations were parties to the original social contract and the attempt to recuperate them as individuals has failed for most of them. Militant elements in the black population—despite the rapid growth of a black middle-class—have largely succeeded in establishing a veto-community that must now be brought into the social compact as one people.

The emancipation of the blacks as one people may demand that our legal structure grant recognition to the rights of "peoples" under our system of government. Claims about the cultural and linguistic rights of blacks are already advanced in the courts. Black power and Black-Panther ideologies argue for collective black action and interests.

The concept of a distinct black people, all of whose members are American citizens, is one that could sadden some selfless enemies of racism—it is one, nevertheless, that would provide an emotional, conceptual, and juridical framework for approaching the problems of the black community as a whole, without precluding the pursuit of individual solutions and of integration made possible by the Warren-Court decisions. Community and racial relations might well be improved in the United States by the extension of juridical and institutional recognition to the separate rights and claims of the black, Indian, and Hispanic *peoples as such*. The unity of the nation and the equality of citizenship could be reinforced by an acceptance of the fact that this nation is made up of separate peoples, and that personal integration does not work for all. For many may indeed prefer to continue their association with the rest of the nation as a separate "people," endowed with group-rights and duties of its own. *Nationality, citizenship, and peoplehood are not interchangeable concepts.*

As we near the bicentennial of the Declaration of Independence, fresh thought should be given to the fate of the black, Indian, and Hispanic peoples in this nation. The integration of immigrants into one nation that characterized the first two centuries of independence should now be followed by the acceptance of blacks, Indians, and Hispanic people as equal partners in our national life. These peoples, who are now the suffering groups in this nation— every member of which is supposedly an equal citizen under the law—consider themselves as distinct peoples, nevertheless. Where appropriate, they should be entitled to reparations, restitution, respect for their cultural rights, and their own institutions for the defense of their rights. Such juridical developments would parallel the legal recognition of labor unions in the last century. But these legal changes would be meaningful only if accompanied by effective measures designed to meet the needs and honor the rights of all our "national peoples." The alteration of expectations, and the new machinery for social change that such juridical innovations may introduce could play a role in improving the fabric of our national life. Imaginative institutional and normative design on a large scale is now urgently required. Our law schools and universities should work on blueprints and models to house the fresh needs and expectations of the nation and provide well-tooled machinery for conflict-control and social change. Institutional and legal designing is now no less urgently needed than urban designing and housing for a rising population. It is needed if only to restore the reality of a society of consent, in which consent rests not merely on the participation of individuals and on procedures of voting, but also on the acceptance of the authority of the state by all relevant communities.

IV

Finally, in considering the "death of the law," attention should be paid to the law-killers, to the *legicides*. It can be fairly maintained that the estrangement of dissatisfied veto-communities is not the only cause for the decline of the authority of the state and its legitimacy. Other factors directly attributable to the state itself do also come into play.

Claims for resistance to legitimate holders of authority have been founded on a number of alternative propositions. Significantly, only a few express a demand for revolution or for a change in constitutional arrangements. Most of the claims are for a *ius resistendi* (right to resist) under a legitimate ruler. They complement the claims to revolution under a tyranny—that is, government without the consent of the governed—but must not otherwise be confused with revolutionary rhetoric. Claims to resist a legitimate ruler distinguish between his legitimacy as a ruler and the legitimacy of his policies and actions. For even the most legitimate ruler could conceivably commit acts abhorrent to the conscience of mankind or fail to perform the most necessary responsibilities of his office. Essentially, these claims fall under eight main headings:

1. On the right of the ruled to resist the ruler, if need be by means of violence, in case of any unlawful usurpation of power (under national or international law) that is not met by effective checks from other branches of the government;

2. On the right of the ruled to resist the ruler when the laws of God or the dictates of morality so require;

3. On the right of the ruled to resist the ruler when fundamental human rights are not protected by the rule of law or when the basic needs of a community are callously neglected;

4. On the right of the ruled to resist the ruler when there is a general and drastic deterioration of legality or pervasive uncertainty about judicial neutrality and the legality of the ruler's own actions;

5. On the right of the ruled to resist the ruler in the absence of effective procedures for peaceful change or of an opportunity to participate in decisions substantially affecting his material interests;

6. On the right of the ruled to resist the ruler in the absence of a meaningful political choice between genuinely different policies;

7. On the right of the ruled to resist the ruler who breaks faith with the people by not honoring his pledges or otherwise betrays the people;

8. On the right of communities to resist the ruler and all other communities when their legitimate vital interests are threatened and when accommodation-procedures have failed.

The legitimacy of these eight claims and the premises on which they rest need not detain us. What does matter is that they are widely entertained. A government that is indifferent or careless of these claims cannot but weaken general respect for law and erode the foundations of its own legitimacy. When, in addition, that government fans the passions of the veto-communities and exacerbates the confrontation of groups, then the prospects for the free acceptance of governmental authority become dim indeed.

On these counts, the actions of some public officials could amount to culpable legicide. These bear detailing, for they illustrate the eight claims and provide a handy guidebook of grievances that frequently explode into civil disorders:

1. the constitutionally unauthorized presidential war in Indochina and the very questionable legality under international law of his prosecution and extension of the war. The gross immorality and doubtful legality of the methods of warfare adopted against the enemy;

2. the infidelity of the administration to the spirit of the desegregation-decisions in a wide range of administrative rulings and its failure to effectively protect the human rights of the black community;

3. the brutal and murderous confrontations between police, guardsmen, and students in the Chicago police-riots, in the Berkeley riots, at Kent State University, Jackson State University, and elsewhere, eroding student acceptance of the authority of the state;

4. the exacerbation of group-tensions by trials widely interpreted as political—that is, designed to repress and brand members of a group rather than to reform, punish, deter, or prevent crime. Such trials appear to run counter to the legitimate functions of nonpolitical criminal justice;

5. the unchecked brutality and lawlessness of some police against student protesters, expressed also in anti-Panther violence. Failure to protect the human rights of youth-communities with a deviant life-style;

   —erosion of faith in the credibility and impartiality of the judiciary in the wake of *ad hominem* attacks on prominent judges, and the damaging controversies surrounding the nomination of Supreme Court justices occurring shortly after the controversy about the performance of Judge Hoffman in the Chicago "conspiracy" trial;

6. erosion of the faith of the legal profession in the neutrality of a judicial philosophy in which competing societal values are admittedly balanced on an unprincipled basis by appellate-court justices, ultimately vindicating faith in judicial power rather than faith in law;

7. timid law-enforcement against organized crime and corporate lawlessness. Corruption in police forces, leading to the nonenforcement of much urban, housing, traffic, and pollution legislation;

8. inefficiency in the capture and trial of criminals, coupled with costly and lengthy trial delays, aggravated by a cruel and anachronistic prison-system;

9. administration rhetoric enhancing expectations about law-enforcement, and the identification of law with order, without sufficient emphasis on social justice, bringing the very concept of law into disrepute among large portions of the citizenry;

10. malignant neglect of the needs of the blacks, slum-dwellers, the old, the underfed, and the poor;

11. neglect of the environment, toleration of industrial-pollution practices, of land-speculations and other commercial ventures destructive of the quality of life;

12. the absence of a meaningful choice of policies between the major national political parties and the manipulated selection of major national political candidates;

13. unresponsive governmental bureaucracies neglectful of the vital interests of communities directly affected by their decisions, in which such communities have little or no meaningful opportunity to participate;

14. the initiation of repressive governmental policies in response to the violence, vituperation, and vandalism of extremist groups;

15. neglect of the claims and needs of veto-communities, in the belief that government need rely only on electoral majorities and favorable opinion-polls.

The seriousness and cumulative impact of all these charges of legicide account in good measure for the disrepair of our domestic legal order.

The eight claims to resist authority help us focus on some of the profound causes for the national malaise. Their utility in this regard may be of greater moment than their acceptability. At a time when authority-structures of all sorts come tumbling down, particular heed should be paid to them. The advent of veto-communities and a developing *ius resistendi* call for a reassessment of our expectations about legal ordering. They demand a new agenda for legal reform and institutional design—a new agenda for legal theory and for the law schools of the nation.

VIRGINIA HELD

Civil Disobedience and Public Policy

Almost every definition of civil disobedience that has been offered in recent years includes at least the requirement that the act of civil disobedience be a violation of law (in some sense) and that the act be performed on grounds of conscience rather than merely for personal gain.[1] Other requirements frequently built into the definition are that the act be public, that the act be nonviolent, and that the civilly disobedient be willing to accept the legal punishment attached to the act. But one can well dispute the claims that any or all of the latter three requirements must be met for an act to be an act of "civil disobedience." What seem justifiably to be represented by them are assertions that acts of civil disobedience which are public, nonviolent, and for which their agents accept the legal punishment are more likely to be morally legitimate

"Civil Disobedience and Public Policy" by Virginia Held. This previously unpublished article is based on a paper read at a meeting of the New York group of the Society for Philosophy and Public Affairs, January 24, 1970. Printed by permission of the author, who wishes to thank Hugo Adam Bedau and Daniel Bell for their comments on the later version; they have disagreed in varying degrees and in various ways with many of the points made here.

1. See, for example, Paul F. Power, "On Civil Disobedience in Recent American Democratic Thought." *American Political Science Review* 64 (March, 1970): 35–47; Hugo Adam Bedau, ed., *Civil Disobedience: Theory and Practice* (New York: Pegasus, 1969); Christian Bay, "Civil Disobedience," *International Encyclopedia of the Social Sciences,* Vol. II, pp. 473–486; Rudolph H. Weingartner, "Justifying Civil Disobedience," *Columbia University Forum* 9 (Spring, 1966): 38–44; Charles Frankel, "Is It Ever Right to Break the Law?" *New York Times Magazine,* January 12, 1964; Hugo A. Bedau, "On Civil Disobedience," *Journal of Philosophy* 63 (October 12, 1961): pp. 653–665. On the other hand, Harrop Freeman's definition of civil disobedience is so inclusive that even legal protests and demonstrations sometimes count as civil disobedience. (Harrop A. Freeman, *et al., Civil Disobedience* (Santa Barbara: Center for the Study of Democratic Institutions, 1966).

or successful than other acts of civil disobedience. These other claims may or may not be well-founded in varying contexts, but they in any case need not, I think, be brought in as part of the definition of civil disobedience.

Consider first the question of whether the act must be public. The purposes of civil disobedience will usually be better achieved by an act which is taken openly and in public, thus distinguishing the act from an ordinary crime. But even were we to define civil disobedience in terms of successful routes to its goals, we would have to observe that one of the more effective ways of bringing about change in the laws is substantial evasion of them, and such evasion can be revealed by polls and studies rather than by public actions. Doctors may perform and women may have abortions, for instance, for highly conscientious reasons, and when the relevant laws are changed it is sometimes more the result of massive private evasion than the result of a few public cases. Hiding political fugitives may be private but conscientious defiance of law. And there appear to be no solid grounds for ruling out, by definitional fiat, from the realm of civil disobedience conscientious obstruction in nonpublic ways of unjustifiable state activities. The appropriate criterion with which to distinguish civil disobedience from crime should be seriousness of commitment in acting on grounds of conscience, not the gaining or avoiding of publicity.

Similar objections can be raised against the other suggested requirements. The purposes of civil disobedience in democratic states will usually be served by limiting the acts taken to those which avoid violence, especially violence to persons. And the principles underlying an act of civil disobedience will frequently be more nearly fulfilled by the disobedient's willingness to accept the legal penalties: he can thereby demonstrate his moral sincerity and his regard for the law in general, though he violates a particular law. However, although these considerations may be highly relevant in deciding whether a given act of civil disobedience is *justifiable* or not, they need not always be thought of as requirements for an act to be classified as an act of civil disobedience.

Questions of where to draw the lines between dissent, civil disobedience, resistance and revolution are not matters of merely formal definition, for innumerable judgments hang on them. To judge, for instance, what kinds of actions government should be expected to tolerate requires terms with linguistic histories. A question which is more nearly one of mere definition, however, is whether a violation of law for the purpose of testing a law considered unconstitutional is an act of civil disobedience. Some writers suggest that such a testing of the law is not, properly speaking, civil disobedience if it is a legitimate claim that what is being taken as law, by a local official, say, really is not "the law," and hence that what appears to be a violation is not one. To challenge a law and to be vindicated is thus not acting "illegally," and to act with a reasonable chance of such vindication is not "disobedience." A more serious question arises when those contesting a law's constitutionality are unwilling to wait for the test to take place, or to desist after the courts have spoken, and act upon their own interpretation of "the law" regardless of how the courts resolve the issue. Massive defiance of segregation laws only later declared unconstitutional in the civil rights struggles of the early sixties, or an unwillingness to accept a Supreme-Court decision on conscientious objection as final, illustrate this kind of civil disobedience.

Some writers contend that even defiance on a large scale, or recalcitrant defiance, if based on the sincere conviction that the law seemingly violated is not really law, are not genuine acts of civil disobedience. Others accord the term civil disobedience to acts based on a different interpretation of the law than that of the courts, and deny that "the law" can be identified with "what the courts decide." Marshall Cohen suggests that almost no acts of civil disobedience are true violations of "law" because those defending them can nearly always claim that they will eventually be vindicated by new interpretations of the fundamental principles embodied in the Constitution.[2] Ronald Dworkin had earlier argued very similarly that anyone refusing to comply with the draft could make a respectable legal case that the Constitution was on his side, and Dworkin suggested that the government should not prosecute these cases because "the law" was not clear.[3] But it seems obvious

2. Marshall Cohen, "Civil Disobedience in a Constitutional Democracy," *The Massachusetts Review*, Spring 1969, pp. 211–226.

3. Ronald Dworkin, "On Not Prosecuting Civil Disobedience," *New York Review of Books*, 10 (June 6, 1968), pp. 14–21.

that *some* time limit must be put on what can be claimed as the time period within which one's position will be vindicated. Otherwise it could be asserted in behalf of any criminal that in a hundred years constitutional interpretations will establish that there are *no* crimes whatever, only demonstrated needs for social education. And one position upon which all writers on civil disobedience are tacitly agreed is that there must be some criteria for distinguishing civil disobedience from at least some forms of crime.

I shall apply the label *civil disobedience of the first kind* to conscientious acts that violate presently valid laws performed by those who can claim and reasonably believe at the time that such acts will be declared legal within something like five to ten years. Such acts can only be considered illegal in the narrowest sense.

Clearly, there are acts of *civil disobedience of a second kind,* in which the person violating the law acknowledges fully that the law he is violating, or another law which he is protesting but not directly violating, is presently valid and not soon to be found unconstitutional. In these cases, because he considers the law to be morally wrong, he intentionally disobeys, or acts illegally to protest, that which clearly *is law.* Examples of this may be found among young men who do not challenge the legality of the draft, but refuse to comply with it on moral grounds, or among those who conceded that it was legal for persons, prior to the enactment of a law against it, to employ white males in preference to equally qualified blacks or women, but who engaged in civil disobedience to protest "existing law" on this matter. In such cases as these, the act of civil disobedience may be an attempt to bring the legal system, itself, to change existing law through new decisions of its own. Or it may be performed with the purpose of influencing the political system to change the law, either the law violated, or some other law which the civilly disobedient considers legally valid, but morally unacceptable.

What I should like to consider more carefully in this paper are acts of *civil disobedience of a third kind,* in which the violation of law as such is entirely incidental, and to consider the justifiability of acts of this kind as forms of political protest. Such acts are intentionally and primarily directed at *political decisions and policies,* rather than at *laws,* either the one directly violated or

some other law, and may therefore be justifiable or unjustifiable
on quite different grounds than acts of civil disobedience protesting
laws.

The most compelling examples of widespread civil disobedience
which we have had in recent years have been in connection with
protests against the war in Vietnam. In some cases, various component acts, when directed at specific political policies and decisions, have been acts of civil disobedience of what I am calling
the third kind. But protest against the war has been so deep and
so general that it has involved all the kinds of civil disobedience
I am trying in this paper to distinguish, its acts ranging from attempts to have pursuit of the war declared unconstitutional, and
efforts to have Congress curb the war through legislation, to application of pressure to policy-makers and Presidents, and to passionate
outcries against war in general.

In his contribution to a symposium in 1961 on "Political Obligation and Civil Disobedience," Richard Wasserstrom deplored
the fact that philosophers had previously, by and large, "tended to
examine only one very special aspect of the problem . . . to consider questions relating to one's obligation to obey the law only
in a context of the conditions under which *revolution* would, if
ever, be justified." [4] A decade later it would be fair to say, I think,
that philosophers have dealt with civil disobedience largely in
terms of protesting *laws*, either directly or indirectly, and have
given much less attention to civil disobedience as a form of protest
against political policies and decisions, among which are many that
cannot be remedied by changes in the law.[5]

The distinction in question is not altogether easy to maintain,
since an effort to apply pressure within the political system to
change a law is a political act, and acts of civil disobedience designed to do so might be classified as acts of the third kind rather

4. Richard A. Wasserstrom, "Disobeying the Law," *Journal of Philosophy* 58
(October 12, 1961): 641.

5. Wasserstrom's own article is an example. Others are Stuart M. Brown, Jr.,
"Civil Disobedience," *Journal of Philosophy* 58 (October 26, 1961): 669–81.
Marshall Cohen, *op. cit.*; Rex Martin, "Civil Disobedience," *Ethics* 80 (January,
1970): 123–37. An exception is Harry Prosch, "Toward an Ethics of Civil Disobedience," *Ethics* 77 (April, 1967), pp. 176–191.

than the second, or a new category might be set up. But since my concern in this paper is primarily with the more purely political kinds of civil disobedience, designed to affect the political system to change political policies and decisions rather than laws, I have not included acts from the overlapping region in this category, and not multiplied the other categories beyond a necessary minimum.

To make the distinctions I am suggesting between kinds of civil disobedience, and to consider the different kinds of justification that may be appropriate for them, one can employ a more general distinction between a political system and a legal system as recognizable sub-systems of a society. This might be represented in some such diagram as the following:

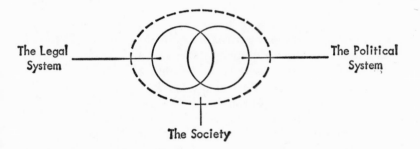

The Legal System ———————— The Political System

The Society

Obviously, the political system and the legal system overlap, the boundaries are unclear, and there are other systems such as the economic one. Many traditional interpretations tend to blur the distinction, seeing both in terms of making law, executing law, and interpreting law. Or they see one system as a sub-system of the other. Most contemporary writers on politics, however, are aware of the serious misunderstandings that result from interpretations that overemphasize the legal, formal, even institutional aspects of political systems.

Without further argument here, then, I assume that we can distinguish political and legal systems, and subject both to moral judgment. I further assume that the characteristic form of justification in a legal system is deontological, the characteristic form of justification in a political system is teleological.[6] Both systems may, then, be seen as moral equals, and moral rivals, so to speak, offering alternative proposals concerning what is morally justifiable. A settlement between claims put forward by both, when they conflict, would have to be made at the level of a moral system, taking into account, presumably, both deontological and teleological factors.

Consider, as an example of a political decision, the establishment by a President, on the advice of his Budget Bureau, and with the pressures of various interests upon him, of budget priorities, and of appropriate sums to be spent on the various activities of the government. Such decisions are among the most important that government can make, yet deciding upon them are not legal matters in any primary sense. Of course the President is such by law, but to consider every decision of a person legally holding an official position a "legal decision" is to collapse politics into legal formalisms. And of course the executive makes its decisions within certain legal constraints. It is required by law to fund programs already mandated by law, such as veterans' benefits, agricultural subsidies, etc. And what Congress does about the President's recommendations will later be law. But although Congress can raise or lower his figures somewhat, the realities of the process are such that the crucial decisions are the President's, and they are primarily political rather than legal decisions. And so on down the line to decisions of the President's advisers, of department heads, of members of the bureaucracy and of regulatory agencies, and so on. Many such decisions have the force of law, but many have political *rather than* legal force. And many of the decisions of political actors such as parties, interest groups, rich donors, and powerful individuals, may be utterly decisive politically, though wholly beyond the reach of the legal system.[7]

It may be that the citizen's objection to a given political decision is not to any of the relevant laws surrounding it, but en-

6. I have developed this argument in an unpublished paper entitled "Political and Legal Justification."

7. The assumption that law "allows" whatever it does not "forbid" cannot be supposed to suggest that the legal system of a society somehow "includes" or "covers" whatever anyone in its does, although some legal theorists write as if one can legitimately think this way.

tirely to the political decision made within these laws. And just as most writers on civil disobedience have rejected the argument of Socrates that whoever accepts a system of laws must accept every law within it, so the time seems to have come for us to move beyond the view that every political decision made within a "framework" of acceptable laws is itself acceptable.

If, in protesting various political decisions, or trying to, protesters violate a *law,* this may well be thoroughly incidental, yet it may be the only, or the most justifiable way for them to register or to act upon an unwillingness to consent to such decisions. Accordingly, some of the requirements that have been suggested for acts of civil disobedience of the first two kinds to be justifiable may require reinterpretation.

One suggestion has been that the act of protest should be directly related to the law that is objected to, so that the law being protested is the one that is violated. Thus if the draft law is thought immoral, an act of civil disobedience that violates it rather than some other law would be far more apt to be justifiable. In some cases we may agree that such a direct relation contributes to the justifiability of the act;[8] as a general requirement, however, a demand for a direct relation makes little sense when the object of protest is a law difficult or impossible to violate, or is the absence of a law. It obviously makes no sense when the object of protest is a political decision or policy, for an individual simply cannot *violate* a budget priority, or an executive decision not to press for a poverty program, or a foreign policy, or a party nomination. But these may be just the things he is most inclined to be civilly disobedient about in the sense of *rejecting,* on moral grounds, the decisions of the political system of which he is a member.

Another suggestion frequently made is that an act of civil disobedience is justifiable only when that which is being protested is remediable by a legal or constitutional change. Thus Stuart M. Brown claims as one of the necessary conditions an act of civil disobedience must meet in order to be justified that "the protests, in the course of which the breaches occur, must be directed at constitutional defects exposing either all the people or some class

8. See Rudolph H. Weingartner, *op. cit.,* p. 42.

of the people to legally avoidable forms of harm and exploitation." [9] And John Rawls cites as a condition for civil disobedience to be justified that "there has been a serious breakdown" in normal democratic processes such that "not only is there grave injustice in the law but a refusal more or less deliberate to correct it." [10]

The kinds of issues raised in what I am calling acts of civil disobedience of the third kind, however, frequently are not issues which can be remedied by constitutional or legal provisions, or issues which the courts could or would adjudicate; they are often not even matters of legal rights or basic liberties, unless the term "rights" is so broadly construed as to lose the clear core of its meaning, and so as to erase the useful distinction between legal rights and political interests. Questions of whether citizens should be provided with a better candidate for office, or a wiser political appointee, or more efficient public services, or a less insensitive foreign policy in a given area, are frequently issues that can not be appropriately dealt with on legal or constitutional grounds. They are often not justiciable issues. Clearly, citizens should not expect the courts and the constitution to make all their decisions for them, and those performing acts of civil disobedience of this third kind might sometimes justifiably choose to bypass altogether the attempt to make a legal defense, or to have enacted new laws. Their purpose would be to act upon their nonacceptance of particular political decisions and policies and their acts could be justifiable on other grounds than if they were acts of civil disobedience of the second kind. In time, ways may be developed to act upon such nonacceptance without actual violations of law, or with some assurance that the political system will not prosecute certain kinds of civil disobedience. Hannah Arendt has recently suggested, for instance, that groups of civilly disobedient persons be accorded a recognition within the political system comparable to that now accorded to organized pressure groups whose lobbyists are permitted and expected to influence Congress.[11] At present, however, short of

9. Stuart M. Brown, Jr., *op. cit.,* p. 677.

10. John Rawls, "The Justification of Civil Disobedience," in Bedau, *Civil Disobedience,* p. 249.

11. Hannah Arendt, "Civil Disobedience," *The New Yorker,* September 12, 1970, pp. 70–105.

illegal action that is subject to prosecution there is often no way for persons to refuse to accept political decisions.

The grounds for the justifiability of acts of civil disobedience of this third kind would be straightforwardly teleological. The arguments here would not be, as they might well be for acts of civil disobedience in conflict with the legal system, that an individual has a deontologically based prima facie moral right not to obey an immoral law, even when the consequences of such an act are unknowable. Nor would they be that the citizen may have a moral obligation to protest a legal situation that is immoral on deontological grounds, *e.g.,* a denial of basic human rights, even when the actual chance of bringing about change through such an act is insignificant.

The questions that would now be most relevant would have to do with whether the act of civil disobedience is likely to bring about good consequences, what values to attach to its possible outcomes, what the probabilities of its effectiveness actually are, and whether the effects that will be produced by it will be more beneficial than burdensome in terms of the general good.

One aspect of civil disobedience of this third kind is that it easily becomes confused with *civil disobedience of a fourth kind,* which consists of illegal acts to protest conditions:[12] poverty, inadequate education and housing, war in general, and so on. Such protests may often be socially useful in dramatizing ugly conditions and changing the climate of opinion within which political decisions are made. Or they may provoke reaction. Sometimes such protests are politically futile, and dissipate attention that could better be focused on recognizable governmental decisions. Of course one must include among governmental decisions and policies those in which it is decided *not* to do certain things. But one should not conclude that there has been a decision worthy of being protested not to do whatever is not done. The political system, like the legal system, has limits. It is only after alternatives for decision can be reasonably clearly formulated that civil disobedience of the third kind, which appears likely to be the most important kind for the 1970s, can be focused sufficiently to be politically effective.

12. Civil disobedience for this purpose is advocated, for instance, by Howard Zinn in *Disobedience and Democracy* (New York: Random House, Inc., 1968).

The framework within which the issues surrounding civil disobedience of this third kind can be considered can be represented,
I think, as follows:

An individual's network of commitments with regard to matters
of public policy includes various possible judgments. The variables
are particular decisions or policies (X), and political decision methods—however simple or complex (M). We then may have the following judgments: "Individual I accepts (or rejects) X"; "Individual I accepts (or rejects) M"; and "M yields X (or non-X)."

A problem arises when an individual finds himself with a set
of commitments such as the following:

    a) Individual I rejects X
    b) Individual I accepts M
    c) M yields X

because it would seem to follow that from b and c we would get

    d) Individual I accepts X.

And of course an individual cannot reject X and accept X at the
same time.

A simple model of the problem would be a case where a given
individual is opposed to having a philosophical association of
which he is a member take a stand on American imperialism.
"Taking a stand" would then substitute for X. But the individual
accepts the method of majority-vote by members for deciding such
matters, and let us suppose a majority of members vote in favor of
taking a stand. What should the individual then do? Should he
change his earlier view that the association should not take a stand,
or is he really not committed to the decision method of majority
vote on the issue?

It would seem that the totality of our political commitments are
in some measure complex versions of the above problem. We have
a set of views on what we are for or against. We accept in general
various component methods of, say, "the democratic process." The
process yields outcomes in conflict with our views. And we face
the moral dilemma of what to do: should we change our views,
give up on various components of "the democratic process," or go
along, grudgingly and with misgivings, with the decisions its
methods produce?

The usual solution that is suggested is that when the democratic procedures yield decisions of which a citizen disapproves, the citizen does not change his *judgment,* but does change his *conduct.* Thus Rawls says that "the right to make law does not guarantee that the decision is rightly made; and while the citizen submits in his conduct to the judgment of democratic authority, he does not submit his judgment to it." [13]

But this does not answer the question of whether the individual *accepts* or *rejects* the decision at a moral level. This is not quite the same as whether he thinks the decision is right, or whether he is planning to do something about it. The question is one of moral consent. And the possibility of separating thought and action, judgment and consent, seems to evaporate at this point. For if an individual sincerely subscribes to a given method of decision, then presumably he must accept what the method yields. But then again, if he is sincerely committed to a position contrary to this outcome, then presumably he must reject it.

What to do about such acceptance or rejection is the next problem. Clearly, moral rejection of a political decision should not always lead to a conclusion that an act of civil disobedience protesting it is justified, for the consequences of such disobedience might often be worse than those of doing nothing. But moral rejection of a political decision does yield at least one good reason for civil disobedience; it is an essential first step. Before the individual can decide whether the good reasons are conclusive for acting upon his rejection through civil disobedience of the third kind, he must settle for himself the problem of moral acceptance or rejection of the political decision in question.

The problem is not resolvable by locating the process of decision in time, and suggesting that the citizen accepts, say, a) and b) *until* he finds out c), and then he changes his mind (or his will) because the problem is one of logical incompatibility.

Richard Wollheim has suggested what might be thought to be a possible solution by drawing a distinction between direct principles, which refer to the morality of actions and policies designated by general descriptive expressions, such as "murder is wrong," and oblique principles, which refer to the morality of actions and poli-

13. John Rawls, *op. cit.,* p. 246.

cies designated by means of an artificial property which they have as a result of an act of will, such as "what is commanded by the sovereign is right." Wollheim asserts that "A ought to be the case" and "B ought to be the case" are not incompatible, even where A and B cannot both be effected, "if one of these judgments is asserted as a derivation from an oblique principle—provided that the direct and the oblique principle are not themselves incompatible." [14] But again, this argument provides no solution to the problem we have been considering, since it supposes that an individual may simultaneously commit himself to principles which yield conflicting recommendations on what he should accept or reject.

What must be concluded, I think, is that—importing a well-known metaphor—the fabric of our commitments faces the tribunal of experience as a corporate body. We can reevaluate the interconnected judgments within it where we choose, and, furthermore, the weave we are willing to accept at any point is our responsibility.

Although most political decision-methods are complex and vague, and may range from "let the president decide on the basis of his superior information," to "if the citizens' committees can't get together, let's do nothing," it may be helpful to examine the issues being discussed through examples of a precise decision method such as a majority vote, without assuming that the vote has, itself, the force of law.

Consider the following political possibilities within the framework outlined above in a) to d):[15] suppose someone reading this paper were to take seriously a proposal for national direct democracy, and to assume a commitment to this method (M) of decision. Then suppose a majority of voters did in fact approve a plan (X) to wipe out poverty by expelling all those with incomes below the poverty line from these United States. Presuming that any reader of this paper would have had an original judgment a) rejecting such a plan, could he suppose that when faced with such a decision

14. Richard Wollheim, "A Paradox in the Theory of Democracy," in Peter Laslett and W. G. Runciman, eds., *Philosophy, Politics and Society*, 2nd series (Oxford: Basil Blackwell, 1962), p. 85.

15. See p. [102].

he would now, because of his commitment to M, abandon a) and accept d)? Surely, he would hang on to a), and revise the network somewhere else. But consider another case: suppose someone were opposed to the building of facilities in a nearby park, thinking trees more beneficial, yet was committed to a majority decision of affected citizens on the matter. If the latter then yielded a decision to build, the individual might well at this point abandon a) and hang on to d).

Most of the interesting issues in the network of our political judgments seem to fall between these two kinds of cases: we know we must revise our commitments somewhere, but it isn't at all clear where.

An obvious candidate for attention is the method in question. Perhaps it does not really have to yield a decision the citizen cannot accept. The citizen can work to try to change its outcome next time, rather than the method itself. And sometimes his objections may be that the result was a faulty application or use of an acceptable method, as when a politician claims to be acting in accordance with the will of a given set of persons, and this claim is false. An act of civil disobedience to protest the misuse of an acceptable method is somewhat comparable to an act of civil disobedience directed at testing a law within a legal system. The claim being made is that the apparent outcome of M is not the "real" outcome of M properly understood.

Still, there will be cases where M really does yield X, but X is morally unacceptable, just as there are cases where a law really is "law," but is morally unacceptable. And this increasingly seems to be what is facing many conscientious persons who accept membership, in some sense, in the American political system, who are committed in general to its decision-methods, but who find themselves unwilling on moral grounds to accept many of the outcomes of this system's decision-processes. At this point, if the citizen is not going to give up a) in the network outlined, he has to reject M itself.

The rejection of various decision-methods in the American political system in the coming decade might take a number of forms. One possible line of attack would be to democratize a system which in many ways only pretends to be democratic. Large numbers of citizens are aware that the military-industrial complex, the ruling elites, the power structure, and all that, manage to bypass the popular will in vast and important areas of activity. Perhaps if existing processes were more genuinely democratic, more participatory, the citizen would not be faced with as many unacceptable outcomes as at present. Proposals for bringing about such change may reflect several main approaches.

First, there may be calls for increased participation in the processes of voting, and in choosing the ways in which governmental programs will be planned and run at local levels. The poverty program, for instance, did make a few efforts to bring about the "maximum feasible participation" of the poor called for in the legislation setting up the program. And nearly all radical and radical-liberal positions include demands for more participation by citizens in the decisions that affect their lives. At other levels, there might be calls for more chances for the electorate to express itself directly, through initiatives, referenda, or related procedures, on various issues.

Secondly, the citizen might be inclined to favor more efficient mechanisms than now exist for aggregating individual preferences, taking the preference-orderings of all individuals on many issues into account, through representative samples or other devices. Here, of course, one runs into the logical problems of deriving a social choice from a set of individual preferences, since from a set of three or more individual orderings of three or more alternative social states, it is not possible to arrive at a consistent collective ordering without resorting to intuitively dubious assumptions, such as an assumption that what would be called the "collective" ordering could be the ordering dictated by the most powerful individual in the group. The well-known paradox of voting illustrates the problem, which has been extensively discussed by Kenneth Arrow and others.

This is a fascinating logical problem which appears to have important political implications. But its immediate political significance may be limited. For the citizen discontented with the existing decision-processes of the United States may well conclude that at levels higher than the local community, both the approaches mentioned above might prove rather disappointing.

The first would tie the holders of power even more closely to popular opinion than they are tied already, and this may be contributing now as much to the citizen's problems as to their solution. A citizen who cannot in conscience accept the decisions of those now in control of political power might find it no less difficult to accept the direct decisions of a regnant majority. Furthermore, voting touches only a limited range of political decisions. Except for the few matters that can be appropriately decided as the result of referenda, voting can only decide who will hold nonappointive office.

As for the second approach, even if the logical problem of aggregating individual preference orderings could be solved, it would be of dubious political benefit. Efficient consumer sovereignty has already proved disappointing enough in the economy. Of course it can be argued that the economy does not really conform to the model of the market mechanism, that giant corporations artificially stimulate popular demands which they then satisfy for profit. But large segments of the economy do in fact reflect consumer preferences fairly accurately, as does the morass of television programming. And the possibilities for distortion would be open to the government as they are to the economy.

The point remains that the citizen may hesitate to make the political system resemble the economic system even more than it does already. And yet this prospect is not remote. A group of important theorists distinguishable as the "political economists" are probably exerting at the present time the dominant influence on political theory, replacing the earlier influence of the "political sociologists." [16] Frequently, they extend to the political system assumptions that seem to be explanatory in the economy, such as the assumption that the individual is a calculating maximizer of his economic self-interest. It is refreshing to encounter their rehabilitation of the notion, sometimes lost by the political sociologists, that people occasionally reason, even if only to calculate their selfish interests. But when the work of the political economists is

16. For a discussion, see William C. Mitchell, "The Shape of Political Theory to Come: From Political Sociology to Political Economy," in Seymour Martin Lipset, ed., *Politics and the Social Sciences* (New York: Oxford University Press, 1969).

taken beyond explanation and turned into normative suggestions that the political system ought to operate along the same lines as the market economy to maximize self-satisfaction, the citizen may do well to start looking for alternative suggestions.

And this brings the discussion back to civil disobedience of the third kind, for it appears to be a feasible way for individuals and groups of individuals to express and act upon their refusals to consent to existing political methods of decision which yield outcomes that are morally unacceptable. Some political decisions are unacceptable not because they do not reflect the accurately calculated selfish preferences of the majority, but because they are wrong. And the way to change them may be to make them more responsive to conscientious rejection of them.

Instead of applying to the political system the assumptions of the market-economy concerning acceptable decision-methods, the citizen might do well to borrow some suggestions from the legal system. Doing so might lead him to take more seriously than he is accustomed to the possibility of developing forms of influencing those with political power through new uses of persuasive argument and the marshalling of evidence, in processes designed to yield political decisions rather than simply further argument. The possibilities for the mediation and arbitration of disputes between citizen groups with reasonable arguments and governmental administrators without them should perhaps not be dismissed too quickly. And the citizen might do well not to recoil automatically from the possibility of the increasing use of experts of various kinds to make and to advocate political decisions. He should not expect popular decisions on all political matters any more than he expects or would like to see juries make all the decisions that are to be made in the legal system. But along with the development of newer political decision-methods must come ways to register and to act upon conscientious rejections of the decisions yielded by these methods in particular cases.

One possibility might be to apply some of the assumptions underlying the relation between workers and management in a corporation to political disputes. Instead of supposing they must persuade the stockholders to persuade management to improve working conditions (a sort of analogue to electoral politics), workers have developed decision-methods that include the possibility of striking, even though their activities in this connection were for many years illegal. Disaffected citizens seem now in the process of developing through civil disobedience what can be thought of as political strikes against units of the political system.

None of these analogies are meant to be more than suggestive. The political system has its own characteristic form of justification; its decisions are normative claims based on expected net good (or least bad) consequences. But the citizen convinced that his own estimate of the good or bad consequences of a political decision are such that he must judge the decision morally unacceptable, may be wise to consider civil disobedience as the appropriate form through which to act upon his moral rejection of such a decision.

Contemporary writers on political systems tend to define authority in terms of what *is accepted*. As David Easton puts it for many of his fellow political scientists: "A policy is authoritative when the people to whom it is intended to apply or who are affected by it consider that they must or ought to obey it." [17] This conception has the interesting implication that when people affected by a policy think they ought not to obey it, it is not authoritative. Argument along these lines should not be expected to win early reversals of legal decisions, but might well be used in efforts to gain reversals of political decisions.

The moral rejection of unacceptable political decisions may take various forms but it must allow for the expression of strongly-felt conscientious dissent in a way that merely voting or being one of those whose preferences are aggregated does not. The person who refuses to accept a political decision, and is willing to risk the penalties attached, can register the intensity of his moral objections, and can address them both to existing decision-processes and to their outcomes.

We have so far tended to think of appropriate limits upon the tyranny of the majority, or of the strong or the rich, in terms of guaranteed rights which even the powerful cannot disregard. But

17. David Easton, *The Political System* (New York: Knopf, 1953), p. 132.

the emphasis on legal rights provides no solution to the political problems which concern political interests[18] rather than legal rights. The political interests, as well as the legal rights, of minorities and the less powerful need protection against overwhelming strength. And for this we need forms of political action that incorporate intensity of objection, and that come into play at the point where justifiable political interests have been unduly disregarded, as the law should come into play where basic rights have been infringed or overlooked.

The issue, however, is often not one of less powerful *versus* more powerful, but of ethics *versus* politics. Forms of action that go beyond the present bounds of legal electoral and interest-group politics, yet do not inflate false hopes about the possible virtues of violent revolution, are in need of development. What I have here called civil disobedience of the third kind appears to be a likely way in which citizens in the decade ahead may try to bring moral judgments to bear upon political decisions.

18. For an analysis of the concept of interest, see Virginia Held, *The Public Interest and Individual Interests* (New York: Basic Books, 1970), Chap. 2.

MICHAEL WALZER

The Obligation to Disobey

According to liberal political theory, as formulated by John Locke, any individual citizen, oppressed by the rulers of the state, has a right to disobey their commands, break their laws, even rebel and seek to replace the rulers and change the laws. In fact, however, this is not a right often claimed or acted upon by individuals. Throughout history, when men have disobeyed or rebelled, they have done so, by and large, as members or representatives of groups, and they have claimed, not merely that they are free to disobey, but that they are obligated to do so. Locke says nothing about such obligations, and, despite the fact that Thomas Jefferson claimed on behalf of the American colonists that "it is their right, it is their duty, to throw off [despotism]," the idea that men can be obligated to disobey has not played much part in liberal political theory.

"Here I stand; I can do no other"—Martin Luther's bold defiance —is hardly an assertion of freedom or a claim to rights. It is the acknowledgment of a new but undeniable obligation. Nor is this obligation often asserted, as it was by Luther, in the first-person singular. In a recent article on civil disobedience, Hugo Bedau has denied the validity of such an assertion, unless it is supplemented by arguments which reach beyond the moral feelings of the individual. "The force of saying, 'I ought to disobey this law' cannot be derived from 'Obeying this law is inconsistent with my moral convictions.'" [1] Perhaps it cannot, and then we must wait upon

"The Obligation to Disobey" by Michael Walzer. From David Spitz, ed., *Political Theory and Social Change* (New York: Aldine-Atherton, 1967), pp. 185–202. Reprinted by permission of the author and the publisher.

1. Hugo Bedau, "On Civil Disobedience," *Journal of Philosophy*, 57: 663 (Oct. 12, 1961).

Luther's further defense before we judge his defiance. But the first
sentence is, in practice, rarely derived from the second. Generally
it follows from an assertion of a very different sort: "Obeying this
law is inconsistent with *our* moral convictions (on behalf of
which we have made significant commitments, organized, worked
together for so many months or years, and so on)." And it can be
argued that, having said this, one can then go on, without offering
additional reasons, to say, "Therefore I ought to disobey." This, at
any rate, is the form that disobedience most often takes in history,
even though additional reasons are usually offered. Men rarely
break the law by themselves, or if they do they rarely talk about
it. Disobedience, when it is not criminally but morally, religiously,
or politically motivated, is almost always a collective act, and it is
justified by the values of the collectivity and the mutual engagements of its members. In this essay I want first to describe the
social processes by which men incur, or come to believe that they
have incurred, the obligation to commit such acts. Then I want,
very tentatively, to say something about the status of the obligations
thus incurred.

The process by which obligations are incurred and the process
by which they come to be felt are not the same, or not necessarily
the same. They are similar, however, in at least one respect: they
are both social processes.[2] They occur in groups, and they can
both occur simultaneously in different groups of different shapes
and sizes. The duty to disobey arises when such processes are more
successful (have greater moral impact) in parties, congregations,
sects, movements, unions, or clubs than in states or churches. This
happens often in human history, but precisely what is involved
when it does needs to be carefully stated.

Obligations can arise in groups of two, between friends, partners,
or lovers. But I am chiefly concerned with those which arise in
groups of three or more, groups of a more general social, political,
or religious nature. These can be obligations to the group as a
whole (including oneself), or to the other members, or to the ideal
the group stands for or claims to embody. In practice, none of

2. The best description of these processes is probably still Émile Durkheim's
Moral Education, trans. E. K. Wilson and H. Schnurer (New York, 1961).

these occur in pure form; obligations are generally, perhaps necessarily, admixtures of the three. But they are often described ex-
clusively in terms of the last. Thus men announce that they are
bound to God or the higher law, and bound "in conscience," which
commonly means as morally sensitive individuals rather than as
members. In fact, however, the very word "conscience" implies a
shared moral knowledge, and it is probably fair to argue not only
that the individual's understanding of God or the higher law is
always acquired within a group but also that his obligation to
either is at the same time an obligation to the group and to its
members. "To be 'true to one's principles,'" Robert Paul Wolff
has written, "is either a metaphor or else an elliptical way of describing loyalty to other men who share those principles and are
relying upon you to observe them." [3] Perhaps this is exaggerated;
clearly people feel that their principles embody what is right, and
there is nothing odd or metaphorical about saying that one ought
to do what is right or what one thinks is right (though it is not
clear that this "ought" implies an obligation).[4] All I want to suggest is that commitments to principles are usually also commitments to other men, from whom or with whom the principles have
been learned and by whom they are enforced.

This becomes clear, I think, if one examines cases in which ideals
are renounced or "sold out." For in all such cases it is individuals
or groups of individuals who feel, and can plausibly be said to have
been, betrayed. To "sell out" is to renounce heritical ideals for the
sake of orthodox ones (but actually, it is generally suggested, for
the sake of material gain) or to desert a small nonconformist group
and join or rejoin society at large. Most likely, as the common
descriptions of this common phenomenon suggest, it is to do both.
"An affront to God and an injury to His congregation"—this is the
way one's former colleagues describe a conversion to religious
orthodoxy. And if God alone can judge the affront, they can rightly
weigh the injury, taking into account the kind of commitment which
had been made, the expectations which had been aroused, the

3. R. P. Wolff, "An Analysis of the Concept of Political Loyalty," in Wolff,
ed., *Political Man and Social Man* (New York, 1966), p. 224.

4. See Alexander Sesonske, *Value and Obligation* (New York, 1964), pp. 20–
23 and *passim*.

ridicule to which they are (or are not) subjected, the possible weakening of their community, and so on.[5] Similarly, but more loosely, an artist who "sells out" by "going commercial" is not merely giving up an ideal; he is giving up an ideal to which others still adhere, and those others are his former colleagues. His offense, in their eyes, is not only his betrayal of Art but also his betrayal of them. He injures the cause of Art, they would claim, both in its ideal form and in its concrete social manifestation.

The individual involved, of course, may be doing or think he is doing no such thing. He may have changed his mind for good reasons. And he may believe (rightly, I think) that there is or ought to be some due process whereby he can announce this change of mind, explain its reasons, and so escape the charge of betraying his former colleagues. But however far his obligations extend, insofar as he is obligated at all it is to other men as well as to ideals. Indeed, to think of the effect of his actions upon the ideal he once espoused, which is surely a necessary part of any due process of renunciation or withdrawal, is also to think of its effect upon those who still hold fast to that ideal.

Obligation, then, begins with membership, but membership in the broadest sense, for there are a great variety of formal and informal ways of living within a particular circle of action and commitment. Membership itself can begin with birth. Then the sense of obligation is acquired simply through socialization; it is the product and most often the intended product of religious or political education, of incessant and unrelenting communal pressure, of elaborate rites of passage, periodic ceremonial communions, and so on. One does not acquire any real obligations, however, simply by being born or by submitting to socialization within a particular

5. Where such judgments cannot be made at all, there is no obligation. And this means that obligations are always shared among men, who must judge one another. "The only obligation which I have a right to assume," wrote Thoreau, "is to do at any time what I think right." But when, in jail, he greeted the visiting Emerson with the famous question, "What are you doing out there?" he clearly implied the existence of a common obligation. Common to whom? Common at least to New England philosophers, one of whom was failing to meet it. Emerson believed the same thing when he spoke in his lecture on the Fugitive Slave Law of the "disastrous defection of the men of letters" from the cause of freedom (*The Complete Essays and Other Writings of Ralph Waldo Emerson* [New York, 1940], p. 867).

group. These come only when to the fact of membership there is added the fact of willful membership. Different groups, of course, define willfulness in different ways, some in such minimal ways that willful membership becomes nothing more than continued membership after a certain age, some in such maximal ways that even formal adherence by an adult is inadequate without a public profession of the faith or a period of intensive participation in specified group activities. Sixteenth- and seventeenth-century protests against infant baptism depended upon a maximum definition of individual willfulness, as did Lenin's attack upon the Menshevik view of party membership. And willfulness can be carried even further. Elaborate tests of would-be members, frightening initiation ceremonies, solemn oaths: these mechanisms of the secret society and the revolutionary brotherhood raise to the highest level the individual's sense of having made a choice of enormous personal significance and thereby assumed the most profound obligations.[6]

In general, well-established groups, especially those like the state, which claim to be coterminous with society as a whole, are likely to defend the minimum definition, assume the commitment of their members, and punish those who disobey. Radical or nonconformist groups, precisely because they cannot make the assumption or guarantee the punishment, are likely to require that commitments take the form of explicit and public professions or acts. Through such professions and acts men can and do take on obligations to disobey the rules of the more inclusive group and also accept in advance the risks of their disobedience.

There is also a third sort of group, not sufficiently organized to make any precise determinations as to the character of membership. Disobedient citizens sometimes say that they are obligated by their membership in the "human community" or by their "solidarity with the oppressed." These obligations, if they exist at all, must be said to be universal (and men have indeed been punished for "crimes against humanity"). But they are generally cultivated in relatively small groups, often themselves loosely constituted, whose members can plausibly accuse one another, but not everyone else, of selling out when they fail to live up to their commitments. Since

6. Eric Hobsbawm, *Primitive Rebels* (New York, 1963), chap. 9; for some examples of secret oaths, see his appendix 13.

the community which is presumably being sold out is not the smaller but the larger group, which does not have any concrete existence and is only an aspiration, it is difficult to see how or whether anyone else can have made a commitment or what his betrayal would involve.[7] It must be said that efforts to enforce such obligations by individuals against their own states, or by groups of states against individuals, are really efforts to create them. Insofar as these efforts win general support, insofar as an entity like "humanity" acquires some "collective conscience" and some legal and institutional structure, real obligations are in fact incurred by membership. Obviously in such an absolutely inclusive community the willfulness of individuals will play an absolutely minimal part. Humanity can indeed be renounced, but only by becoming a criminal of the very worst sort, by turning oneself into what Locke called a "savage beast." At the present time, since no group exists which can satisfactorily define crimes against humanity, "savage beasts" are necessarily punished ex post facto, not for betraying humanity, but in the hope of creating a humanity whose members are capable of recognizing treason.

The state itself can sometimes be imagined as an ideal or potential community, obligating its members to oppose those authorities who act legally but (it is thought) immorally in its name. Thus those men who disobey the commands of a collaborationist government after military defeat, or of a satellite government after some less formal capitulation, often claim that their state has been betrayed and that they are obligated by their previous membership and driven by their patriotism to resistance. But they cannot claim that all their fellow citizens are similarly obligated. In the aftermath of such struggles, if the resistance is successful, active collaborators may be punished (the legal basis for such punishment is unclear enough), but nothing can be done to those who merely declined to join the fight.[8] They had never incurred any duty to do so. On the other hand, those who did join and subsequently deserted can rightly be said to have broken tangible and morally significant commitments. Thus a leader of the French Resistance,

7. Sesonske, *Value and Obligation*, p. 107.
8. Henry L. Mason, *The Purge of Dutch Quislings* (The Hague, 1952), chap. 2.

defending the excution of a deserter: "In the Maquis each man had chosen his own lot, fashioned his destiny with his own hands, picked his own name. Everyone had accepted in advance and without question all possible risks." [9] The same obviously cannot be said of Frenchmen in general.

To insist that obligations can only derive from willful undertakings is to restate the theory of the social contract. This has very interesting consequences given the rough typology of groups and kinds of membership just outlined. For contract theory clearly applies best to those sects, congregations, parties, movements, unions, and clubs in which individual choices are made explicit, acted out in some public fashion. It is most useful in discussing what are commonly called secondary associations, less useful (though by no means of no use at all) in discussing larger groups like states and established churches or vague and inclusive entities like humanity. Indeed, if the contract is taken at all seriously, it is difficult to avoid the conclusion that groups in which willfulness is heightened and maximized can rightfully impose greater obligations upon their members than can those catholic religious and political associations where membership is, for all practical purposes, inherited. Of course, inherited membership is often seconded by voluntary participation; in such cases the sense of obligation, as well as the obligation itself, is probably strongest of all. But even participation is likely to be more active and willful and so a more satisfactory token of continuing consent in nonconformist than in established and socially orthodox groups. Day-to-day procedures will be less conventionalized, the modes of participation and communion less habitual. In short, it is possible to conclude from contract theory, as Jean Jacques Rousseau did, that small societies are (generally) morally superior to large ones. For is it not the case that obligations incurred within some Protestant sect, derived from an explicit covenant, and sustained by a continual round of activity, ought to take precedence over obligations incurred in society at large, derived from "tacit" consent, and sustained by mere residence or occasional, largely passive, participation? I do not want to attempt an answer to that question

9. Guillain de Benouville, *The Unknown Warriors* (New York, 1949), p. 220.

immediately; perhaps there are good reasons for the negative answer conventionally given. But I do want to make two points: first, that obligations are in fact incurred within groups of these different sorts; second, that the conventionally assigned relative weights of these different obligations are not obviously accurate.

The duty to disobey (as well as the possibility of selling out) arises when obligations incurred in some small group come into conflict with obligations incurred in a larger, more inclusive group, generally the state. When the small group is called a secondary association, it is being suggested that there is no point at issue here. Secondary associations ought to yield without argument, conflict, or moral tension to primary ones.[10] This is true only of associations clearly secondary, that is, with purposes or ideals which do not bring them into conflict with the larger society. Rotarians cannot sell out.[11] But there exist in every society groups which may be called "secondary associations with claims to primacy." Serious conflict begins when groups of this sort are formed and their claims announced. But here a crucial distinction must be made: these claims can be of two very different kinds. Some groups announce what are in effect total claims. Their members are obligated, whenever commanded, to challenge the established legal system, to overthrow and replace one government with another, to attack the very existence of the larger society. These are revolutionary groups. There are others, however, that make only partial claims. They demand that the larger society recognize their primacy in some particular area of social or political life and so limit its own. They require of their members disobedience at certain moments, not at every moment, the refusal of particular legal commands, not of every legal command.

It is worth insisting upon the great difference between such groups and between the assertions they make, for defenders of state sovereignty often confuse them, arguing that any challenge to constituted authority is implicitly revolutionary and any group which

10. S. I. Benn and R. S. Peters, *The Principles of Political Thought* (New York, 1965), chap. 12.

11. People who accuse trade-union leaders of selling out are, in effect, accusing them of acting like leaders of secondary associations, the implication of their accusation being that the union (or the labor movement generally) is something more than secondary.

claims to authorize such challenges necessarily subversive. They thus assign the labels "rebel" and "subversive" to all sorts of people who explicitly reject them. When this is done by officials of the state, the labels often turn out to be accurate, since the men who originally chose not to revolt are eventually forced to do so in self-defense. But there is considerable evidence to suggest that the state can live with, even if it chooses not to accommodate, groups with partial claims against itself. The disobedience of the members of such groups will be intermittent and limited; it is unlikely to be conspiratorial in any sense; it does not usually involve any overt resistance to whatever acts of law enforcement the public authorities feel to be necessary (unless these are radically dispro-portionate to the "offense"). Such disobedience does not, in fact, challenge the existence of the larger society, only its authority in this or that case or type of case or over persons of this or that sort. It does not seek to replace one sovereign power with another, only to call into question the precise range and incidence of sov-ereignty. This is not revolution but civil disobedience, which can best be understood, I think, as the acting out of a partial claim against the state.

Limited claims against larger societies can themselves be of two kinds. They can involve assertions that the larger society cannot make demands of a certain sort against *anyone,* or they can involve claims for exemptions for the members (and the future members) of the smaller society. When a man refuses to register for military service, without challenging state authority in any other sphere, he may be saying that the state cannot require anyone to fight on its behalf or to fight this or that particular sort of war, or he may be saying that people like himself cannot be so required. The second statement generally accompanies acts of conscientious ob-jection, which represent only one kind of civil disobedience.

The larger society can always recognize the claims of smaller groups and so relieve their members from the burdens and risks of disobedience. Indeed, the historical basis of liberalism is in large part simply a series of such recognitions. Thus the limited disobedience of religious sectarians was transformed into mere non-conformity when the state decided to tolerate the sects. Tolerance required a limit on the power of the state, a recognition that with regard to religious worship any church or sect could rightfully claim primacy. Contemporary conscientious objectors are also tolerated nonconformists, but here the tolerance is of a different sort. It is a recognition of the claims of a particular type of person (or of particular groups of people) rather than of the claims of any person (or group) in a particular area. There is no necessary logical restriction on either type of toleration: the state could withdraw all its claims from an infinite number of areas, or it could add to every one of its laws a provision specifying that conscientious disobedience cannot be punished.[12] But few states seem likely to move very far in either of these logically possible directions, doubtless for good reasons.

What is the situation of men who join groups with limited claims to primacy in states where such claims are not recognized? It is a situation which political phiosophers have never adequately described—though Rousseau surely understood the possibility of divided allegiance and divided men and bent all his efforts to avoid both. Locke provides a convenient outline of the possibilities more generally thought to be available: (1) A man can be a *citizen;* this involves a full recognition of the primacy of his society and its government. Certain areas are set beyond the reach of the government, but in such a way as to bar any possible obligations against it. There are only rights and ultimately, so far as action goes, only one right, the right of rebellion. Hence, (2) a man can be a *rebel,* seeking to overthrow and replace a particular government and its laws. These are the only two possibilities available to members of the larger society. But Locke suggests two further options for those persons who do not wish to be members: (3) A man can be an *emigrant,* willfully withdrawing from the larger society and physically leaving its territory. Emigration is the only due process through which social obligations can be renounced, for the rebel is still bound, if not to his government, then to society itself. Finally, (4) a man can be an *alien* who, having left the society of his fathers, fails to commit himself to any other and lives here or there at the discretion of the public authorities. An alien, for Locke, has obligations, for he is afforded protection

12. Bedau, "Civil Disobedience," p. 655.

within some particular society and tacitly consents in return to obey its laws. He presumably has rights, at least in theory, since rights are natural. He must even possess, I think, the right to rebel, though it is not clear that he possesses this right as fully as citizens do: he cannot protest if his consent is not asked to government or taxation. This appears to be the single most important difference between aliens and citizens.

Now the member of a group with partial claims to primacy falls into none of these categories. His loyalties are divided, so he is not in any simple sense a citizen. He refuses to call himself a rebel, and with good reason, for he seeks no total change in the government, no transformation of state or society (though he would surely claim the right to rebel, in Locke's sense, given the conditions under which Locke permits rebellion). He is not an emigrant, since he does not leave, though joining such a group may well constitute a kind of internal emigration. He is not an alien, for while an alien can always leave, he cannot demand to stay on conditions of his own choosing.

Yet the situation of such a man—obligated to obey because of his membership in a larger society, obligated to disobey (sometimes) because of his membership in a smaller one—is, for all its tensions, very common in history and has often been fairly stable over long periods of time. It is the situation of any person who, like Sophocles' Antigone, retains strong tribal or clan loyalties while becoming a member of some (almost any) political order.[13] It is virtually institutionalized in feudal systems.[14] It was lived through with extraordinary intensity by early modern Protestants and has been lived through since with greater or lesser intensity

13. The conflict in Sophocles' play is, of course, between primary groups. In general, conflicts between groups of relatives or friends and the state take forms similar to those described above, especially in modern times when such alliances tend increasingly to be voluntary. E. M. Forster's statement that "if I had to choose between betraying my country and betraying my friend, I hope I should have the guts to betray my country" is roughly analogous to the sorts of assertions sometimes made on behalf of groups. But it is an extreme statement and has reference to exceptional cases. Most often, the choice is between betraying one's friends (or colleagues) and disobeying the laws of one's country. Antigone's act is not treason, in any usual interpretation of that tricky term. Forster, Two Cheers for Democracy (New York, 1951), p. 78.

14. See Marc Bloch, Feudal Society (Chicago, 1961), chaps. 9–17.

by a considerable variety of religious groups (including Roman
Catholics, for Rousseau the visible embodiments of double obligation and moral division)—even in liberal societies, which have
recognized some but not all the claims of pious brethren of this
or that persuasion. It was the situation of European socialists during the period when their parties and movements had ceased to be
revolutionary but had not yet accepted the status of secondary associations. (Otto Kirchheimer describes German Social-Democracy
as a "loyalty-absorbing counterorganization." [15] It is often the situation of trade unionists, especially when their country is at war. It
is the situation today of all those persons who object to military
service on other than the permitted religious grounds. It is, despite
considerable confusion, increasingly the situation of many members
of the American civil-rights movement.

What all these oddly assorted people have in common is this:
none of them admits without qualification the political sovereignty
or moral supremacy of the larger society of which they are members. None of them absolutely denies that sovereignty or supremacy. They are, then, partial members; they are simultaneously
partial emigrants, partial aliens, partial rebels. The very existence
of such people—even more, their obvious moral seriousness—
ought to call into question the conventional description of citizenship as involving an absolute commitment (it is sometimes said,
"under God") to obey the laws. Surely such a commitment will
never be found among every one of those persons who consider
themselves, with reason, citizens of the state. For the processes
through which men incur obligations are unavoidably pluralistic.
Even or perhaps especially in a liberal society, which allows considerable room for divergent groups and recognizes many of their
claims, what might be called the incidence of obligation is bound
to be uneven, the obligations themselves at least sometimes contradictory. Unless the state deliberately inhibits the normal proc-

15. Otto Kirchheimer, *Political Justice* (Princeton, N.J., 1961), p. 9. Trotsky
takes an even stronger position, with regard not to Social Democracy but to the
working class, and then draws an important conclusion: "In all decisive questions, people feel their class membership considerably more profoundly and
more directly than their membership in 'society' . . . The moral norm becomes
the more categorical the less it is 'obligatory' upon all" (Irving Howe, ed., *The
Basic Writings of Trotsky* [New York, 1963], p. 378).

esses of group formation, and does so with greater success than has ever yet been achieved, it will always be confronted by citizens who believe themselves to be, and may actually be, obligated to disobey. As J. N. Figgis wrote: "The theory of sovereignty . . . is in reality no more than a venerable superstition . . . As a fact it is as a series of groups that our social life presents itself, all having some of the qualities of public law and most of them showing clear signs of a life of their own." [16]

Many political philosophers have insisted that there exists a prima facie obligation to obey the laws of the most inclusive organized society of which one is a member, that is, for most men, the state.[17] This is not unreasonable, so long as the state provides equally to all its members certain essential services. It is not unreasonable even though the state maintains a monopoly of such services and tolerates no competition, for it may be that the monopoly is itself essential to the provision of the services. But the existence of a prima facie obligation to obey means no more than that disobedience must always be justified. First explanations are owed to those of one's fellow citizens who do not join in, who remain obedient. I think it can be argued that membership (that is, morally serious membership) in groups with partial claims to primacy is always a possible explanation.

But I want to attempt a somewhat stronger argument than this, loosely derived from the preceding discussion of the uneven incidence of obligation in any larger society. I want to suggest that men have a prima facie obligation to honor the engagements they have explicitly made, to defend the groups and uphold the ideals to which they have committed themselves, even against the state, so long as their disobedience of laws or legally authorized commands does not threaten the very existence of the larger society or endanger the lives of its citizens. Sometimes it is obedience to the state, when one has a duty to disobey, that must be justified.

16. J. N. Figgis, *Churches in the Modern State* (London, 1914), p. 224. See also G. D. H. Cole, "Conflicting Social Obligations," *Proceedings of the Aristotelian Society*, n.s., vol. 15 (1915), and "Loyalties," *ibid.*, n.s., vol. 26 (1926).
17. See, e.g., W. D. Ross, *The Right and the Good* (Oxford, 1930), pp. 27–28; and discussion in Richard Wasserstrom, "Disobeying the Law," *Journal of Philosophy*, 57: 647 (Oct. 12, 1961).

First explanations are owed to one's brethren, colleagues, or comrades. Their usual form is an argument that physical security or public health or some other such necessity of the common life—which the smaller groups cannot supply, which is actually supplied by the state—is being threatened or is likely to be threatened by particular acts of disobedience, however limited their scope. This, of course, is precisely what is asserted (usually by an official of the state) in every case of disobedience, but it is not necessarily asserted rightly. Indeed, there is very little evidence which suggests that carefully limited, morally serious civil disobedience undermines the legal system or endangers physical security.[18] One can imagine situations in which the acting out of partial claims might encourage or inspire the acting out of total claims. But the two sorts of action remain distinct. It may be necessary for a man contemplating civil disobedience to worry about the possibilites of revolutionary violence, but only if such possibilities actually exist. It is by no means necessary for him to reflect upon the purely theoretical possibility that his action might be universalized, that all men might break the laws or claim exemptions from them. For his action implies nothing more than that those men ought to do so who have acquired obligations to do so. And the acquiring of such obligations is a serious, long-term business which is not in fact undertaken by everybody.

The state can thus be described as a purely external limit on group action, but it must be added that the precise point at which the limit becomes effective cannot be left for state officials to decide. For them, the law must be the limit. At the same time, it must be the claim of the disobedient members that the law is overextended, that its sphere ought to be restricted in some fashion, that this activity or this type of person should be exempted, at

18. It is often enough said that disobedience even of bad laws undermines the habit of law abidance and so endangers that fundamental order upon which civilized life depends. But I have never seen this argued with careful attention to some particular body of evidence. In the absence of such an argument, I would be inclined to agree with David Spitz that there are clearly *some* laws obedience to which is not required for the maintenance of social order. Even more important, perhaps, there are many laws which can be disobeyed by *some men*, without prejudice to social order (Spitz, "Democracy and the Problem of Civil Disobedience," *Essays in the Liberal Idea of Freedom* [Tucson, Ariz., 1964], pp. 74–75).

this particular moment or for all time. There can be no possible judge of this disagreement. All that can be said is that the moral seriousness of the disobedient members is evidenced in part by their respect for those genuine goods the state provides not only to themselves but to everyone. To argue that the state does not provide such goods at all, or that it denies them entirely to particular sections of the population, is to justify, or to try to justify, unlimited and uncivil disobedience, that is, revolution. Revolution always requires (and generally gets) some such special justification.

There are two other ways of describing the state which appear to argue against the claim that disobedience can ever be a prima facie obligation. The first is to insist that the state is itself a group, that its members too are willful members who have incurred obligations of the most serious kind. It was the original purpose of social-contract theory to uphold just this conception of the state. But there are serious problems here. Since for many men there are no practical alternatives to state membership, the willfulness of that membership seems to have only minimal moral significance. A theory like Locke's requires the argument that one can always leave the state; residence itself, therefore, can meaningfully be described as a choice. That argument has some value—it may even be true that more people move across state frontiers now (though not always voluntarily) than in Locke's time—yet one cannot always leave, and so we would be wrong, I think, to base the weightiest political obligations on the non-act of not-leaving. There is a better way of describing the willfulness of state membership: that is to take very seriously the possibility of joining secondary associations with limited claims to primacy. Such engagements represent, as I have already suggested, a kind of internal emigration, and so long as the processes of group formation are open, and whether or not the frontiers are open, they offer real (though partial) alternatives to state membership as it is conventionally described. It is not the case, of course, that whoever fails to seize upon these alternatives thereby declares himself a member of the state and accepts all the attendant responsibilities. But membership is established as a moral option by the existence of alternatives. Thus, the possibility of becoming a conscientious objector establishes the *possibility* of incurring an obligation to fight in the army. But if the groups within which men learn to object are repressed by the state, that possibility disappears, for in one important sense at least the state is no longer a voluntary association.[19] Only if the possible legitimacy of countergroups with limited claims is recognized and admitted can the state be regarded as a group of consenting citizens.

But the obligations of citizens to the state can be derived in yet another way: not from their willfulness but from its value. "If all communities aim at some good," wrote Aristotle, "the state or political community, which is the highest of all, and which embraces all the rest, aims, and in a greater degree than any other, at the highest good." [20] Obviously, groups which aim at the highest good take priority over groups which seek lower or partial goods. There are two major difficulties, however, with Aristotle's description. First of all, it is not the case that the state necessarily embraces all other communities. A state with an established church and no legal provision for religious toleration obviously excludes a dissenting sect. Groups with universalist or international pretensions, like the Catholic church or any early twentieth-century socialist party, necessarily exclude themselves. Political or religious communities which oppose war are in no simple sense "embraced" by states which fight wars. It is precisely the nature of secondary associations with claims to primacy that they cannot and do not exist wholly within the established political or legal frame. Second, while the state may well provide or seek to provide goods for all its members, it is not clear that these add up to or include the highest good. Perhaps they are goods of the lowest common denominator and only for this reason available to all, for it may be that the highest good can be pursued only in small groups—in pietist sects or utopian settlements, for example, or, as Aristotle himself suggested, in philosophic dialogue. In any case, men do not agree as to the nature of the highest good, and this fact is enormously significant for the processes of group formation. Groups are formed for a great variety of reasons, but one of the chief reasons is to advocate or act out ("without tarrying for the mag-

---

19. I argue for the pluralist basis of conscientious objection in the sixth . . . and of citizenship in the tenth [essay in *Obligations*, Cambridge, 1970].

20. Quoted in Benn and Peters, *Principles*, p. 315, and discussed, pp. 315-325.

istrate," as a late sixteenth-century Puritan minister wrote) a new conception of the highest good, a conception at which the state does not aim, and perhaps cannot. To form such a group or to join one is to reject Aristotle's argument and renounce whatever obligation is implied by it. I fail to see any reason why this is not an option available to any morally serious man.

In the argument thus far, I have attached a great deal of weight to the phrase "morally serious." Obviously, the term is not easy to define, nor the quality easy to measure. Yet frivolous or criminal disobedience cannot be justified by membership in a group. There are obligations among thieves, but not prima facie obligations against the state. This is true, first of all, because the activities of thieves endanger the security of us all. But it is also true because a robbers' gang does not make claims to primacy. Thieves do not seek to limit the authority of the sovereign state; they seek to evade it. But there is nothing evasive about civil disobedience: a public claim against the state is publicly acted out. This willingness to act in public and to offer explanations to other people suggests also a willingness to reflect upon and worry about the possible consequences of the action for the public as a whole. Neither of these by themselves legitimate the action; but they do signal the moral seriousness of the group commitment that legitimates it.[21]

Frivolous disobedience can also never be a duty, and so groups that do not encourage an awareness of their members of the purposes and actions to which they may become committed cannot commit them. Awareness of this sort would appear to be required by social-contract theory; even the notion of tacit consent implies that there exists some knowledge of the duties being incurred. Nor, it seems to me, are the requirements of the theory entirely satisfied if such knowledge is but glimpsed at one brief moment in time. Continued awareness, a kind of shared self-consciousness, is necessary before the consent and participation of individuals carry sufficient moral weight to establish obligations—or, at any rate, to establish such obligations as I am trying to defend. A morally serious member of a group with partial claims may, then, be described as follows: he joins the group voluntarily, knowing what member-

21. Secret societies, if they are not criminal, are implicitly revolutionary; the moral seriousness of their members must be signaled differently.

ship involves; he devotes time and energy to its inner life, sharing
in the making of decisions; he acts publicly in its name or in the
name of its ideals. Such a person—not any person—is obligated to
act as he does, unless he is given good reasons why he ought not
to do so.

The problem of civil disobedience needs to be placed squarely
in the context of group formation, growth, tension, and conflict.
There is a sociology of disobedience, which has greater relevance
for philosophy than has generally been thought; it helps establish
the proper units of analysis. Now these units doubtless have their
limits, for it is true that there come moments when individuals
must make choices or sustain actions alone—or rather, and this is
not at all the same thing, when they must endure the anguish of
loneliness. The state always seeks to isolate its disobedient citizens,
because it is far more likely to bend their wills to its own if it can
break the cohesion of the group which initially planned the disobedience and convince its members that they are members no
longer. But this only suggests that the men who run prisons are
always very much aware of the sociology of disobedience. Surely
philosophers should be no less so.

The heroic encounter between sovereign individual and sovereign state, if it ever took place, would be terrifyingly unequal. If
disobedience depended upon a conscience really private, it might
always be justified and yet never occur. Locke understood this very
well, for even while he proclaimed the right of individuals to rebel,
he recognized that "the right to do so will not easily engage them
in a contest, wherein they are sure to perish." [22] Rebellion, he
thought, is only possible when it engages "the whole body" of the
people. But clearly, rebellion and, even more, civil disobedience
are most often the work of groups of much more limited extent.
Clearly, too, it is not the mere individual right to rebel, unchanged
in groups large or small, that sustains the enterprise but, rather,
the mutual undertakings of the participants. Without this mutuality, very few men would ever join the "contest"—not because
of the fear of being killed but because of the greater fear of being
alone. "This is what is most difficult," wrote Jean Le Meur, the

22. John Locke, *The Second Treatise of Government*, par. 208.

young French army officer who was imprisoned for refusing to fight in Algeria, "being cut off from the fraternity, being locked up in a monologue, being incomprehensible." And then: "Do tell the others that this is not a time to let me down." [23]

All this is not to suggest that there is anything unreal about individual responsibility. But this is always responsibility *to someone else* and it is always learned *with someone else*.[24] An individual whose moral experiences never reached beyond "monologue" would know nothing at all about responsibility and would have none. Such a man might well have rights, including the right to rebel, but his possession of the right to rebel would be purely theoretical; he would never become a rebel. No political theory which does not move beyond rights to duties, beyond monologue to fraternal discussion, debate, and resolution, can ever explain what men actually do when they disobey or rebel, or why they do so. Nor can it help us very much to weigh the rightness or wrongness of what they do.

23. Jean Le Meur, "The Story of a Responsible Act," in Wolff, *Political Man*, pp. 204, 205.
24. Individual integrity, honor, or "authenticity" is different from this, though it is sometimes described, metaphorically, as responsibility to oneself. In the ninth [essay of *Obligations*], I discuss possible conflicts between obligation and personal honor.

ALFRED G. MEYER

Political Change through Civil Disobedience in the USSR and Eastern Europe

The communist states of Soviet Russia and Eastern Europe have undergone significant, at times dramatic, political transformations within the last two decades; and since each of these systems has changed at its own pace and in its own direction, the universe of European communist systems by now is quite heterogeneous. Nonetheless, it may be possible to make a few generalizations that will still apply to all of them.

I

Communist regimes come to power, not necessarily by revolution, but with the aim of carrying out a revolution, that is, a thorough change of the entire social, economic, and political system. This involves destruction of established institutions and the erection of new ones—a phrase written lightly, even though it implies gigantic efforts, conflicts, convulsions, and hardships. The methods used by communist regimes in their attempts to effect such revolutions-from-above (to use Stalin's phrase) are well-known. They include the attempt to subject the entire organizational and associational life of the society to control by the ruling party; the thorough reeducation of the population in the spirit of the party's ideology, which seeks to establish its authority in all areas of human thought; and the marshaling and mobilization of all material

"Political Change through Civil Disobedience in the USSR and Eastern Europe" by Alfred G. Meyer. From Pennock and Chapman, eds., *Political and Legal Obligation* (New York: Atherton, 1970), pp. 421–39. Reprinted by permission of the author and the publisher.

and human resources for the tasks to which these regimes give top priority—national defense, political stability, and rapid industrial growth. The form of the resulting polity is bureaucratic; its style, paternalistic, with the father figures shifting from moralistic sermonizing to vengeful, punitive coerciveness, to grudging offers of rewards for good performance.

The theoretical justification for this paternalism is provided in the communist theory of state, elaborated by Lenin, Stalin, and their successors, and codified in the textbooks on Marxism-Leninism. According to this doctrine, the communist state is just and rational; it therefore is entitled to obedience by all citizens. It has these qualities because it is ruled by the Communist party; and this party asserts as axiomatic truth that it fully and truly represents the interests of all the people. Therefore, there neither is nor can be any conflict between the rulers and the ruled, and all authority is by definition self-imposed. Since the communist state is a state of all the people and for all the people, any work done or sacrifice made for it by the individual is in the interest of that individual. Indeed, there can be conflicts between individual and public interests only in the false imagination of unenlightened or immoral citizens.

The image sketched here obviously implies a system that tolerates neither deviant behavior nor deviant thoughts. Indeed, it frowns on any yearning for privacy or escape; and its architects have a compulsive need for assurances that their society is obedient, disciplined, and fully united behind its leaders. Manifestations of heterogeneity, not to mention conflict, are regarded as disturbances.

Strains nevertheless appear in all communist societies. The old order cannot be destroyed and replaced at will; instead, it fights for survival. The peasantry resists collectivization, actively or passively; national sentiments remain alive; scientists assert their knowledge against party ideologists; religious practices survive. In short, the national culture offers resistance to the bureaucratic revolution-from-above. Within the ruling bureaucracy, meanwhile, the infighting and internal politicking that troubles all giant organizations inevitably appear, together with such age-old phenomena as inefficiency, corruption, and the abuse of authority—all causing pain to both the political elite and the masses of the population. Further strains arise from the fact that communist societies develop a class structure or a stratification pattern or, if the expression be preferred, pyramids of rank, authority, affluence, power, status, and so forth, in which competition for advancement is sharp, and those not rising as high as they think they should may come to regard the entire social order as inequitable. Strains and growing pains notwithstanding, communist regimes may nonetheless reach their immediate goal, which is the industrialization and modernization of their relatively underdeveloped societies. When they do this, the Communist parties that have hitherto manipulated their societies with relative abandon (subject to the reservations expressed above) gradually find themselves confronted by complex, heterogeneous societies, sensitive to arbitrary tinkering, but sometimes unresponsive and at other times nervously overresponsive to coercion, high-handedness, and other paternalistic methods; societies containing many professional elites with intellectual conventions and ethical codes of their own and with strong ties to professional colleagues across the ideological borders. It is obvious that all the strains I have listed engender dissent as well as pressure for change. But the confrontation of modern industrial society with a political elite of the Stalinist type generates by far the strongest of these urges. In this case the pressure is for political change, for restructuring the political system from system-building to system-management, from bureaucratic revolutionism to liberal conservatism, from command to interest aggregation.

The communist systems of the USSR and Eastern Europe have felt pressures in this direction to a greater or lesser extent for the last fifteen years or more. But the counterpressures have also been very strong. Resistance to the changes that seem necessary are of various types. One of them is ideological, which means nothing else than that the practices of Stalinism were codified into a doctrinal catechism and thus elevated to solemn dogmas. Although the figure of Stalin has been removed from its pedestal, and his body from its resting place *ad dexteram patris,* the forms and institutions and style of his rule have lingered on persistently, partly because they were deeply engraved in the ruling ideology. The ideology, in turn, is reaffirmed with stubborn persistence by the established political elite, which is a product of the Stalinist era, learned how to rule under it, is not likely to retrain itself for the rather different functions that seem called for today, and regards all and any pressures for reform as threats to itself and to the entire system. One might add that bureaucratic establishments in general tend to become immobilistic; or one could argue that bureaucratic rulers as well as paternalistic authoritarians harbor deep suspicions against all manifestations of "spontaneity," i.e., all activities they themselves have not organized and inspired. Change, and indeed all policy and activity, is to be initiated at the top, not at the bottom or even in the middle layers, of the system. Hence in the communist polities being examined here politics is repressed and muted; debate is not quite legitimate, because, theoretically, all intellectual problems are supposed to be solved by reference to codified authority. Pressures for change are totally illegitimate; and individual or group claims against the system are not allowable either. Against abuses the individual may and indeed should complain; and for the relief of undue hardships or inequities the system provides numerous safety valves. Moreover, each citizen and every conceivable collective body is expected to show initiative in carrying out their many assignments. On the whole, however, dissent and the expression of interests, to say nothing of pressure for political change, are severely discouraged. Moreover, the *range* of permissible action is more restricted than, say, in the United States, almost as if the guiding rule were, "Whatever is not expressly permitted is forbidden." To state this formally, in addition to a codified legal framework of rights, duties, and prohibitions, the European communist systems operate with a restrictive framework of custom, usually referred to as socialist morality, which they enforce with the help of both peer group constraint and political authority. To the American academic observer the difference between communist and Western systems seems to be very great, although it may well be that the American ghetto dweller, the migrant farm-worker, or the long-haired youth holding "straight" values in contempt finds unwritten law as restrictive and as harshly and capriciously enforced as socialist morality in the USSR.

Having noticed the constrictive framework of communist countries, in which the authorities seek to endow all human endeavors

with political significance, so that all life activities become matters
of public policy, one may be surprised by the variety of ways in
which the citizens of these countries do express dissent or dissatisfaction and may even seek to bring about changes. (I will leave
aside for the moment the question which, if any, of these actions
fall within the fabric of "civil disobedience.") The observer may
be even more astonished to find that some of these methods have
been in use throughout the history of these societies, even during
the reign of Stalin. Libermanism was voiced by some economists
as early as the 1940s. A play sharply critical of the Soviet military
establishment was written and staged during World War II (*The
Front* by Korneichuk). György Lukács never quite ceased arguing in
favor of a turn toward enlightenment and intellectual tolerance.[1]
We have dim knowledge of strikes and demonstrations through most
periods of these countries' history. Pasternak wrote his passionately
antirevolutionary novel during the chilliest years of the Stalinist ice
age. Indeed, the years 1946–48 in the USSR, and the years 1952–53
in Hungary and Poland were periods of profound, prolonged, and
widespread stirrings of dissent. With full information we would
doubtless learn that there has been change in the frequency with
which such sentiments were expressed. But relative acquiescence
reigned only during a few brief periods when sharp repression
temporarily shocked the people into silence. In the USSR, these
years of almost total absence of dissent might be 1935–39, 1948–49,
and 1951–52; in Eastern Europe (except for Yugoslavia), the only
period of this kind was 1949–52.

An exhaustive list of all kinds of deviant behavior manifested
in communist countries would have to include various actions that
are of no interest to us here, such as corruption; the systematic
and deliberate violation of legal or other rules practiced by administrators, managers, and other people wielding public authority
for the purpose of fulfilling their assignment or doing their job
well; or, more broadly, the ever-present tendencies toward informal
organization and informal behavior which are familiar to all students of complex organizations and bureaucratic management.
These well-known patterns of rule-breaking, without which large

1. His article written on the 170th anniversary of Lessing's death and published in *Szabad Nép*, February 15, 1951, veils this message only very thinly.

administrative structures could not function, are mentioned only in order to show that underneath the façade of purposeful orderliness there is plenty of individual or group autonomy, initiative, competition, and at times even pressure for change. The boundary between the evasive tactics of bureaucratic officials and instances of civil disobedience may be very unclear. Another type of behavior outside the scope of this chapter is the clever use of existing rules and frameworks for ends not intended by the regime, as the use of grain for feed by collective farms in periods when the price difference between grain and livestock makes this profitable for them, as happened in the USSR in 1953–54. This practice contributed to a grain shortage which in turn was one of the reasons for Khrushchev's campaign to till the virgin lands of Kazakhstan. Yet another kind of deviancy of little interest here is criminality and asocial behavior such as juvenile delinquency, alcoholism, absenteeism, and disrespect for authorities,[2] even though a sharp increase in the frequency of any such behavior is likely to be interpreted by party leaders as a sign of protest and a symptom of political crisis or unrest, hence as some sort of public desire for change. Still, these many types of deviancy will be neglected here because our concern is for deliberate expressions of dissent and dissatisfaction and deliberate moves for some alteration in the system.

I shall make a list of typical forms of deliberate dissent, ordered somewhat roughly according to the degree of their severity or illegality. They range from clearly legal and permitted acts through words or deeds that may be legal, but violate socialist morality or party discipline, to clearly illegal statements or activities. The lines of demarcation here too are not rigid, and depend on changes in the political climate. What is permitted today may have been illegal a few years ago; what is beyond acceptable behavior in Poland may today be quite proper in Hungary. Indeed, what can be done quite openly in Science City may lead to immediate arrest in Novosibirsk, a few miles away. In displaying such variety of legal and moral frameworks, the communist world is no different from ours.

2. A most surprising token of contempt for authority I myself observed in a Soviet city some years ago was the attempt of a police officer to detain a young lady for some offense. The girl resisted arrest and managed to escape because bystanders in large numbers came to her aid.

Individual citizens, who feel they have cause for complaint against officials or agencies (of a relative subordinate rank), can and do write to a wide choice of authorities in the party, the press, the parliament, or other representative assemblies, and to law enforcement agencies or inspectorates to call attention to the alleged misdeeds; and it is clear from all the evidence we possess that such complaints are investigated. This channel of complaint is perfectly legal, widely used, and often not very effective, because the deeper causes of dissatisfaction are immune to such complaints either because they are related to policies to which the regime is firmly committed or because they are imbued with an authority which the complainant dare not touch.[3]

A slightly more daring and also more effective way of resisting authority is the maintenance of behavior patterns and the expression of ideas that do not entirely fit into the mold of the "socialist man," or the good communist. As I have hinted above, communist societies harbor subcultures that have resisted assimilation, and whose members continue to live according to patterns not entirely liked or approved of by the parties. Some of these are traditional in origin, such as ethnic groups or religious communities; and these have maintained their own way of life with surprising success. At times they resist assimilation or destruction openly and boldly: gypsies still refuse to settle down or give up their unproductive work; believers may openly wear religious symbols or demonstratively attend services. In 1966, some of the celebrations of the Polish millennium turned into mass demonstrations of loyalty to the Roman Catholic Church. Other subcultures are of more recent origin; for instance, the many professional and scientific elites loyal to their own professional ethics, or the new youth culture which renounces the values of a careerist, "straight" society, and dares to show signs of such renunciation. We know of numerous other ways

3. It is generally understood that a substantial portion of complaints voiced through these and other safety valves provided by communist regimes is in fact inspired, suggested, or planted by the party authorities themselves. This is most obvious in the case of official humor magazines (*Krokodil, Szpilki, Eulenspiegel,* and others), that point the arrows of their satire at those abuses or failures which the party wishes to eliminate. Yet some of these magazines have come under fire because they overstepped the limits of permissible criticism. Cf. the 1947 denunciation of Zoshchenko and the criticism leveled ten years later at the editors of *Eulenspiegel.*

of showing dissatisfaction with what the regime offers: consumer strikes against shoddy goods; readers' boycotts of officially approved literature; or those subtle but unmistakable demonstrations that take the form of applauding, booing, or remaining silent at the wrong places during a public performance of some kind, be it a play by Schiller or the oratory of someone cloaked with authority. When this is done by party members it can be a serious offense against party discipline. For there are occasions when the party expects every loyal member to speak up, be it for the purpose of self-criticism or for the purpose of denouncing someone whom the party condemns. In 1947 it took several months of pressure before Varga's colleagues publicly rejected his views. And when Pasternak was publicly repudiated, hardly any major Soviet writer joined in the ritual.

The various professional subcultures seem to have an intensive intellectual and social underlife, if we can generalize from what we know about the culture of artists, writers, and scientists in these countries. These professions are deeply divided into factions according to their commitment to, or rejection of, establishment ideas and policies. The dissenters or radicals know that they face a variety of publics which can at times be manipulated. They may form protective alliances with like-minded people in other subcultures or become their clients, as for instance the artists who create in nonofficial styles and survive in the USSR because the scientific elite buys their works and in this fashion sponsors them. For this reason, Soviet graphic art, which can be sold for lower prices than canvases, seems to be more avant-garde than painting; while sculpture remains the most traditional art form. In Eastern Europe I made friends with an artist whose statues were done in Stalinist style, but his pastels were unorthodox in both style and content.

The liberal-radical subculture I am talking about seems well organized even though split into wings and cliques. It behaves like a clique against the outside world of officialdom, even though it also has multiple and close connections with it. Its various factions may have their own hangouts and, in periods of relative freedom, their own journals, even if they are only obscure journals published in provincial towns. In 1956–57, the Polish radicals had

Po Prostu; the radical liberals wrote for *Przegląd Kulturalny*; for
the establishment liberals the party created *Polityka*; the party itself
spoke through many other newspapers and journals; and the far
right spoke through the Soviet publications *Pravda, Kommunist,*
and *Voprosy Filosofii.* Today, the radical right need not publish
abroad, but the radical left does in *Borba* (Belgrade), *Kultura*
(Paris), *Grani* (Frankfurt) and many other outlets.

Among the institutions serving the liberal-radical community,
there is an intensely active black market in books and works of
art; equally active circulation of unpublished manuscripts, unauthorized, semiprivate concerts, readings, or exhibits; and, most
illegally, the circulation of mimeographed agitational material. At
the time of the Siniavsky-Daniel trial in the Soviet Union, an entire
White Book, prepared by people friendly to the defendants, circu-
lated widely and was finally published abroad. It contained letters
that had been written to, but not printed by *Izvestiia* and *Litera-
turnaia Gazeta,* summaries of defense testimonies before the court,
and unpublished letters to the party Central Committee, the court,
and other authorities. In the wake of this much-publicized trial
there has been a series of other cases before Soviet courts as well
as punitive administrative actions, all dealing with a continuing
wave (or wavelet) of dissenting and protesting activities, including
public protests against the Soviet military intervention in Czechoslovakia in August 1968.

There is thus vivid traffic in information and ideas, including
open protest; much of this traffic doubtless flows up into the highest
circles of the party leadership. Of all this the Western observers
receive only occasional samples; some material leaked out by the
liberal or radical community through its friends abroad, some of it
from the party press itself, for instance, in reports about scientific or
professional congresses, or in some derogatory remarks made by a
party leader.[4]

Incidentally, the liberal-radical subculture seems to have its
special heroes. These are the victims of administrative reprisals,

4. An impressive collection of such documents can be found in *Problems of
Communism,* vol. XVII, no. 4, pp. 31–114, and vol. XVII, no. 5, pp. 24–112;
the latter issue includes interesting samples of protest poetry, fiction, and
criticism.

alumni of concentration camps and torture rooms. Some of these victims of Stalinism, according to recent observers, seem to enjoy an almost saintly prestige, are respected even by the authorities, and apparently enjoy a certain measure of fools' freedom. They are in the forefront of dissent and reform movements. It is even more remarkable to observe how many top-ranking party leaders owe their rise and their initial popularity or charisma to the fact that they have done time in the jails of Stalin or the little Stalins of Eastern Europe. This is true of several people in the highest councils of the Czech, Hungarian, and Polish parties.

The respect and relative permissiveness with which the party tends to treat these heroes of the liberal and radical communities, even when they are no longer in positions of authority, indicate that these subcultures must be examined in their interaction with the establishment. The first observation to be made here is that the liberal intelligentsia and the officialdom test each other continually, the liberals seeking to stretch, and the party bureaucrats to restrict the bounds of permissible behavior. The radical subculture lives a more pronounced underground existence, even though technically many of its activities are not illegal either. After a few dadaist "happenings" in Budapest, in 1967, the participants, or some of them, were taken to police headquarters and warned not to stage any more, so that the next happening was already an act of defiance, although still not clearly illegal.[5] Neither is it illegal to resign from the Communist party, a step taken by a number of leading Polish writers in the fall of 1957 and by several other groups in Eastern Europe since then. But it is rightly regarded as a slap in the face of the establishment, almost as embarrassing to the regime as suicide. It is amazing how sensitive communist elites are to suicide on the part of their leading citizens, and how suicide therefore becomes a mode of civil disobedience, seemingly more shocking to communist leaders than the ritual self-immolation of Vietnamese or American dissenters is to their political leaders.

Less destructive means of protest include strikes and work stoppages. The almost total cessation of Soviet, Hungarian, and Bulgarian writers to submit manuscripts in the late months of 1957 was a

5. This statement is based on several informants who participated in these "happenings."

silence strike which seems to have been well organized and to have
hit the party very hard. People can strike by not showing up at
compulsory meetings, as the students of Humboldt University did
in the summer of 1957 when the new State Secretary in the Minis-
try of Education, recently appointed to tighten control over the
universities, came to address them and faced a hall full of empty
benches.[6] Or people can show up where they are not supposed to,
as the townspeople of Turza (Upper Silesia), whose parish priest
the party threatened to replace by another; the people came out in
a protest demonstration, and the priest stayed.[7] Authorized meetings can be used for unauthorized purposes, like the famous cele-
bration of the tenth anniversary of the "Polish October" which
took place at the University of Warsaw in October 1966. At this
meeting, another interesting variant of showing dissent was practiced
when mimeographed copies of Gomulka's programmatic speech of
ten years before were distributed, only to be seized by the authorities as, presumably, a subversive document. Needless to say, it
would be equally subversive to quote some of Mao's writing today,
just as it would at least be tactless today to quote Lyndon B. Johnson's 1964 election speeches dealing with United States policy in
Asia. And, of course, it would be even more subversive in the communist world to take Marxism seriously. For that offense, Kuron
and Modzelewski today are in jail.

The most ludicrous example of illicit behavior doubtless is the
offense of doing good deeds without prior authorization, not so
much because it implies criticism of the establishment, but far more
because it is a manifestation of spontaneity. A nice example is
furnished by the eager beavers of the Tashkent Komsomol who,
bored with the routine activities of their organization, decided
to show their enthusiasm and their commitment to communist
morality by undertaking a variety of constructive community proj-
ects. A suspicious public prosecutor, possibly sensing a conspiracy,
began to investigate. Some arrests were made. In the end the sus-
pects were released. But the Komsomol authorities expressed their

---

6. See F. L. Carsten, "East Germany's Intellectuals," *Problems of Communism*, VI: 6 (1955), 50.

7. M. K. Dziewanowski, "Communist Poland and the Catholic Church,"
Problems of Communism, vol. V, no. 3 (September–October 1954), 7.

fury at the impudence of these young people's independent activity.[8]

For the sake of completeness, let me briefly mention the recurrent instances of mob action and violence in the communist countries. With the possible exception of the riots in Soviet labor camps, 1952–54, all violent upheavals known to me began as unplanned and peaceful demonstrations and were turned into bloody uprisings only by the repressive acts of the police or (in the case of Hungary) intervention forces. This applies to the working-class riots of Berlin, Plzen, and Poznan as well as to the violent Polish riots in October 1957, after *Po Prostu* was closed down. The case of Hungary in 1956 is somewhat more complex. Here a genuine revolutionary situation developed as soon as the Hungarian troops refused to open fire on the demonstrators. Had the Soviet troops not interfered, the disorders would most probably have led to an overthrow of the communist regime. In some of the labor-camp revolts, as well as in Hungary, and also in Poland in October 1956, unarmed demonstrations and police violence were followed by the emergence of participatory democracy, taking the form of action committees (soviets).

In surveying the entire phenomenon of dissent and pressure for change in these countries, one is struck by the great fluidity of the limits between permitted and forbidden modes of expressing dissatisfaction or criticism. The capriciousness with which official humor (humor magazines, cabaret, circus clowns) is treated by the party is a token of its ambivalence in this respect. Even more telling instances of insecurity and ambiguity are the frequent disagreements in high circles, or the sudden changes in judgment: a book highly praised by *Izvestiia* may be condemned by *Pravda* on the same day. Such things happened even under Stalin.

The overall impression is that people no longer quite know what is and what is not proper to say. Kuron and Modzelewski are in jail for making statements that are far less provocative than the editorials of *Po Prostu* or even *Trybuna Ludu* ten years earlier. Adam Schaff has been fired for saying things that some years before were considered establishment ideology. When Mihajlov went to

8. The incident is discussed in *Komsomolskaia Pravda*, November 10, 1956, p. 2.

jail the first time, it was for expressing sentiments that were less radical than those printed in *Praxis* at the same time. What Tarsis, Siniavsky, and Daniel have written is no more radical than the works of Wazyk, Dudintsev, or Solzhenitsyn, or of Bulgakov, whose books are now being published in only slightly censored versions. One gets the impression that communist leaders often are more shocked by what is said than what is done, that they fear words more than actions, and thus will tolerate many an unorthodox practice as long as no one calls attention to it. Sanctions are imposed not on what is illegal but on what the bureaucrats feel to be threatening— threatening to them, or to the establishment, or to the moral, cultural, and political stereotypes by which the establishment lives. Similar fluidities in the boundaries between permitted and intolerable behavior may exist in many other societies.

II

I shall now comment on what I have written so far by asking which of these manifestations of dissent, if any, ought to be regarded as acts of civil disobedience. I shall then conclude with an attempt to assess the effectiveness of any such acts, that is, with some remarks about the place of civil disobedience in the communist societies of Russia and Eastern Europe.

In his recent encyclopedia article on the subject, Christian Bay defines civil disobedience as an act of public defiance of a law or policy enforced by established government authority.[9] The defiance should be premeditated, open, and ought to be conceived as an example that others might follow. It should be known by the perpetrators of the act to be illegal or of contested legality. Bay emphasizes the care and deliberation with which practitioners of civil disobedience must limit both the ends and the means of their acts. He sees the principal aim of such defiance as educational: civil disobedience strives to change public and official perceptions about what is and what is not illegitimate. Moreover, he argues that the aim of such defiance should always be conciliatory, never divisive.

9. Christian Bay, "Civil Disobedience," *International Encyclopedia of the Social Sciences*, vol. II, pp. 473–87.

The emphasis here is on a meticulous adherence to moral precepts, and the outlook for success appears very gloomy. Civil disobedience, according to Bay, results from a painful weighing of evils against each other (disobedience versus violence; personal defeat versus the sin of inflicting harm). The mood is one of existential despair; typically it is Camus who becomes the major spokesman of the philosophy of civil disobedience. Indeed, the wish not to win seems at times to motivate Bay:

> Countless individuals in the course of history have chosen to shed their blood rather than compromise in matters of faith or conviction. It is arguable, however, how many among them should be considered spokesmen for civil disobedience. Their acts of defiance may in many cases have been instinctual; even visceral, rather than premeditated; their goals may at times have been unlimited—say the salvation of mankind; and their means may have not always been *chosen*. . . . Not every brave and for the time being nonviolent true believer is practicing civil disobedience when defying the law of the government; one would at least require of him a reasoned determination not to repay injustice suffered with new injustice inflicted once victory has been won.[10]

As if a victory, once won, did not have to be secured!

The pessimism inherent in this interpretation seems to be based on the assumption that morally intolerable political systems cannot be reformed without violence, but that violence must under all circumstances be foresworn. By itself, the first assumption would convert its adherent into a revolutionary. But the revolutionary sentiment is turned into existentialist pessimism by a concentration on the means-ends dilemma. This dilemma then turns into the axiom that reforms are impossible as long as they are necessary, it being understood that they become unnecessary should they ever become possible. Meanwhile, one must try the seemingly impossible, which is moral suasion through demonstrative self-sacrifice or carefully chosen acts of defiance. The rejection of revolution as an alternative, moreover, is derived not only from the means-ends dilemma, but perhaps even more from an important if residual

10. *Ibid.*, p. 475.

commitment to the given system: some of its details may be evil, but its basic structure, or at least the principles by which it allegedly operates, are accepted, and a totally different system is either not desired at all or is considered unattainable under the given circumstances. Hence civil disobedience is loyal opposition in a system which is reluctant to tolerate any opposition and manifests no great willingness of change itself. One of the reasons why the prospect of success for this kind of opposition is so gloomy is its dependence on publicity. Yet many courageous acts of defiance are either given the silent treatment or are distorted into violent, subversive acts by the establishment media. Many of the protests voiced in the communist world reach us despite the authorities because they somehow find their way into the foreign press, though the Soviet public at large is not informed about them. Civil disobedience nonetheless does work under some circumstances; there are occasions when one can work on the enemy's conscience. There may be forces within the society (interest groups, classes, factions within the political elite) that can be aroused by acts of civil disobedience; finally; there may be cases in which the authorities lose little by giving in, or when it would be more costly for them to suppress civil disobedience than to yield to it.[11]

In trying to match acts of defiance in the USSR and Eastern Europe with this definition of civil disobedience, I was surprised at how many of the activities summarized above fit this definition, and how neatly Christian Bay's specifications apply to the situation of dissatisfied elements in these countries. First, it should be stated that, to a limited degree, the ruling elites of communist countries have become sensitive to moral suasion. These are political systems committed to a systematic ideology, over the interpretation of which they seek to exercise most rigid control; but they have not quite succeeded. Not that their vulnerability in this regard ought to be overstated. More important, the existentialist mood of civil disobedience, in which evil is carefully and painfully weighed against evil, in which whatever you do gets you into trouble, so that at times the only thing that still counts is the morally correct stance— this mood seems to be an apt portrayal of the perception which

11. See the discussion of *ahimsa* in E. Victor Wolfenstein, *The Revolutionary Personality* (Princeton, N.J.: Princeton University Press, 1967), p. 288.

dissenting intellectuals have of their own communist systems. The moral tone of political discourse, especially after Khrushchev's so-called secret speech of 1956 had torn the mask off Stalinism and exposed its moral bankruptcy, forcibly strikes anyone surveying the rise and fall of reform movements in communist countries. The only circles in which one finds a similar preoccupation with morality in politics in the Western world are the radical student movements of today. One must add that the radical and liberal intelligentsia in the communist world have been thoroughly politicized, and they try to calculate finely the remotest consequences of their actions. Nowhere in the world does dissenting political activity seem to be so self-conscious and deliberate as in these countries. Furthermore, these spokesmen for reform usually are very careful to limit their demands; their opposition indeed is loyal most of the time, and they try hard to push for reform without provoking the authorities into retaliatory action. More and more they appeal to the rights granted them by the constitutions allegedly guiding their political systems. Like the civil rights movement, which began by asserting rights which full citizens take for granted (like being served a bowl of soup at a drugstore lunch counter), the liberal-radical protest movement (if one can speak of a movement) in the communist world has begun to insist on the actual exercise of rights formally granted by existing laws. Indeed, the appeal to formal norms of the polity, the insistence on adherence to rules, laws, and constitutions, in short, the legalism and constitutionalism of the dissenters is the trait in the pattern of Soviet and East-European protest phenomena most likely to impress the foreign observer.

The care with which dissenters in the communist world have limited their demands is one argument in favor of classifying their activities as civil disobedience, as defined by Bay. One might object that it is fear rather than a moral calculus which defines the limits of dissent in authoritarian societies. But this objection is unconvincing because of the spectacular growth of courage, the conquest of fear, shown by increasing numbers of dissenters in that part of the world. This new spirit of defiance and fearlessness, manifested in words and deeds, gives the protest movement in the communist world a profoundly moral character and in this sense, too, renders Bay's definition of civil disobedience applicable to their activities.

The people I have discussed do not fight for narrow personal gain nor group advantages. Theirs is an activity of self-abnegation. They are imperiling their careers, their comfort, and their liberty for a purpose they see defined in highly moral terms. They speak for the nation or even for mankind rather than for a group or a class; or at least they think they do. Clearly we are discussing people who are bearing witness to their ideals.

The success of all this pressure seems, at first glance, to have been tremendous. The extension of freedom, or more exactly the widening of the range of permissible behavior, over the last fifteen years has gone much beyond anything that most Western students of communist societies would have dared to imagine. There have been serious setbacks, and the pace of liberalization differs markedly from one country to another or even from one realm of human endeavor to another. Still, the overall change has been dramatic. The boundaries of permissible or tolerated behavior have been stretched perceptibly in life styles, entertainment, art, and science; in contact with foreign countries and the absorption of Western influence, even in such sensitive fields as philosophy and social science; in the critical examination of the past and even the present; in economic relationships; and, in Yugoslavia and Czechoslovakia, even in political life.

The list could be extended at will, to include the dismantling of much of the police apparatus, the decollectivization of agriculture in Poland, the greater emphasis placed by economic planners on consumer satisfaction, changes in the Polish, Hungarian, and Czech regimes, Khrushchev's de-Stalinization campaigns, and the alleviation of some of the worst conditions in forced labor camps in the wake of riots, honors paid by the authorities to victims of their own policies and indeed to the rebels against this oppression. The successes have indeed been remarkable.

It is impossible, however, to determine which of these changes are the result of conscious and deliberate pressures for reform and which of them might have come about in any event, without pressure. It seems safe to say that all meaningful reform has come about only when dissent and civil disobedience found a responsive echo in some strategic force within the society, be it a significant group like the scientific community, an entire class like the workers, or a faction within the ruling party. At the same time, when change has resulted from demands made more spontaneously and inarticulately by broader masses of the population, it is doubtful whether we can examine with sufficient exactness what role civil disobedience or intellectual rebellion played in triggering reform. Some day, perhaps, monographs may be written about some specific reform in which the relationship between grassroots demands and articulation of conscious interest can be examined. The material now available is not sufficient for this.

The argument up to this point about the success of civil disobedience and its functional equivalents in the USSR and Eastern Europe might seem to place me among those specialists who foresee continued liberalization in this area of the world. Indeed, strong arguments may be advanced to support this view. The simplest argument is that the wheel of reform cannot easily be reversed, that a society once freed from excesses of repression will not submit to it again. A more sophisticated argument is that a modern industrial society is too complex to be run by command and repression. Repression is regarded as dysfunctional to modern society. Its sharpest manifestation, terror, is often interpreted as a primitive but effective mobilization device for societies in which other means for mobilizing inert populations and resources are scarce. But it becomes counterproductive after a certain level of modernization has been reached. In turn, this interpretation of the functions of terror is related to widely accepted theories of progress (usually called development or modernization), according to which economic development leads to a more and more stable social and political equilibrium of the modernizing society.

These arguments do not convince me, however, and I cannot therefore commit myself to this view. In fact, recent developments in various parts of the world, including our own, but most spectacularly the Soviet intervention in Czechoslovakia (August, 1968), suggest that this view may be too facile and optimistic. Terror, authoritarianism, and repression may have important functions even in mature industrial societies, long after the mobilization phase is over. Or, if indeed they are counterproductive, that may not necessarily imply an inevitable trend toward liberalization. Dissent and heterogeneity may be more unsettling and threatening in mature industrial societies than they are in modernizing ones; the need to preserve law and order may become so overwhelming that strong repression becomes routine. In the communist polities of the Soviet Union and Eastern Europe, such a reassertion of authoritarianism does not even require political change; instead, it would merely mean a continuation of the political legacy of Stalinism. What I have argued, however, is that even in such authoritarian regimes dissatisfied groups can find means short of violence, and involving appeals to moral principles, that may have long-range effect.

PHILIP BERRIGAN, S. S. J.

A Priest in the Resistance: An Interview

Q. *Could you describe what your sacramental life as a priest has been in the past, and how it might have been changed by your experience in jail?*
A. Well, I think that my sacramental life has always been largely conventional. Even in Newburgh in 1965, when I was already seriously into the peace issue, I used to say mass daily, and I would go to confession pretty much on a weekly basis. And this continued on into my Baltimore days, because I was in a parish where people needed the Eucharist every day. And then, too, because it was quite an advanced parish, both liturgically and socially. On Sundays a lot of whites would come, not only from the city itself, but even from out of state. They would be progressive Catholics looking for good liturgy and a good homily, or they'd be peace people looking for a more serious orientation for their own lives, and wanting to discuss issues. Today I go to confession maybe once every three months. Of course, there's an entirely new approach to confession now, and this has affected all Catholics. The orientation in my confession is largely how I might have failed in my responsibilities toward people, especially those who are involved in communities of witness, who are on the borderline of risk, and who are in the process of commending themselves to the Gospel in a very serious way—which, according to the present jargon, means an entirely new life style. How I have failed in my responsibilities there, and of course one's failures are always manifold, because it's an entirely

"A Priest in the Resistance: An Interview." From *Prison Journals of a Priest Revolutionary* by Philip Berrigan, compiled and edited by Vincent McGee (New York: Holt, Rinehart and Winston, Inc. Copyright © 1967, 1968, 1969, 1970 by Philip Berrigan. Reprinted by permission of Jerome Berrigan and the publisher.

new dimension, it's very, very difficult, it's very abrasive. You're dealing with such a wide spectrum of ideology—political analysis, conscience, emotiveness, all these things. The ideal preparation would be to sit with a friend and talk it out. But the only person I've found that I could do this with would be my brother Dan. Failing the opportunity to do that with him on a frequent basis—though I suppose I could get the opportunity if I really attempted to organize it—I go to a Jesuit confessor in the center of Baltimore. And I go through a rather conventional thing.

Q. *What does the sacrament of penance mean to you, as an experience or as a need?*

A. Well, of course, I still believe profoundly in the dimension of grace, which is imparted through the sacrament. And all of the allied things on which grace depends—atonement, retribution, sacrifice, and the development of new attitudes toward the future, the making of a new present in order to secure a better future. I still believe very powerfully in these. And they suggest what I'm looking for.

And the Eucharist is still quite central to my life. I usually either offer the Eucharist with friends, or else I offer a very truncated and very reflective Eucharist in my room, at my desk, almost daily. And that means a long scriptural meditation, and a very, very short public-oriented offertory, and then the consecration.

Q. *How would you describe your discipline of prayer?*

A. I conceive of prayer as a reflection upon the divine operation in the human community, and the relationship of God to man, and out of that, of man to man. Reflections upon this, and dealing with whatever insights have come from the New Testament, mostly; and renewed dedication in terms of responsibility to the needs of the human community, which I conceive of increasingly in universal terms.

Q. *How has your stay in prison affected your sacramental life?*

A. I think it might have clarified it a great deal in the sense that one is thrust into a new role in prison, one is forced to grope for a new justification for one's presence in prison. You have to rationalize it because you have to extract hope from it, and this is a very living need. It isn't so much a straight-ahead, ongoing process as it is a matter of being humbled, starting all over, looking for maybe the right questions. Not that I had any doubts in prison about the rightness or correctness of it for me. In fact, maybe I have arrogance enough to assume that it has a relevance for a lot of other people; that it *is* a public necessity, in fact. I've never had to do too much fumbling in that regard; yet at the same time I went through a dynamic of thought which thrust me more fully into the question of the meaning of prison—what can be accomplished there, what it does mean outside, what connection it has with the movement.

Q. *Do you find celibacy tougher in jail, or no tougher, or the same as out?*
A. It's tougher out. Because of the hypersexuality that's operating today, and the kind of sexual confusion that's operating in the peace movement, there are many more challenges outside, I would say, than if one were in jail, just single-mindedly going ahead with the business of trying to resist in some faint way, writing, or working with people. Outside it becomes much more difficult. Because in the oddest sort of way, movement people associate sexuality with humanity. But I'd like to stress that Dan and I feel that celibacy is crucial in the priesthood as an aid for revolutionary life style. We believe this very strongly, especially because we have made strong overtures to the other Christian communities in terms of action, in terms of awareness, political response, and all the rest, and gotten largely nowhere. With very, very good men. With men who have acted in a variety of ways in the past. And almost invariably the question of family obligations comes up, children, etc. So we feel celibacy can be a great freedom in a public forum.

Q. *Do you see prison in a sacramental sense—you know, in the old catechism definition of a sacrament being an occasion of grace? Is that how you see the example of your witness in prison?*
A. Yes. Being imprisoned for one's convictions is a Christian phenomenon above all, and also highly relevant politically. I would go so far as to say that if someone (not necessarily myself), if only one man were in prison for the right reasons, although challenged by an entire country, it would still make a contribution of grace and new life in ways that cannot be imagined.

Q. *In your decision to go to jail and witness, are you saying that the central message of Christianity is redemption through the ultimate powerlessness of the crucifixion?*

A. Yes, most definitely. You have the example of Christ, and before that the whole prophetic experience of the Old Testament, and, of course, the Acts of the Apostles. Despite all the failures, there is a constant Christian tradition for two thousand years, leading to resistance to the Nazis, and more recently, the resistance against the French government during the Algerian crisis. For the committed Christian, there is a moral example, a religious guideline—almost a matter of doctrine. In addition, there is the political relevance of witnessing in jail, because there's not going to be basic change, there's not going to be human revolution—or even structural revolution in the sense that Bishop Helder Camara speaks of it—unless consciences are moved. And we don't know enough yet about how to move consciences, and this has its political aspect. And I've come to the conclusion that this can only be done by risk, by what people understand as suffering—what they are not willing to endure themselves. It can only be done by giving up one's freedom, which in a country like our own is only less precious than life itself. Americans have a phobia against jail because we have less of a tradition of resistance, and less of a tradition of jail experience influencing the national consciousness.

Q. *Let's speak a bit about Bonhoeffer, whose witness in jail has become a great example to many of us. Has it ever struck you that Bonhoeffer, within the very small nucleus of resistance in Germany, was in a small minority in pledging himself willing to kill Hitler himself? There were only about ten percent of the people involved in the German resistance who were actually willing to commit violence, and Bonhoeffer, the one eminent pastor in the group, was one of the ten percent. How would you reflect upon that, in terms of Christian nonviolence?*

A. I would say that this was the mistake of a very, very good man who, because of the massiveness of the machine against him, was led into desperation, and abandoned the main premises of his own basic message by falling into this trap. Bonhoeffer's example in this regard should be contrasted with that of another Protestant, Paul Schneider, who died under Hitler and preserved intact the message of nonviolence right up to his death. To me, he is a greater man than Bonhoeffer. I have read some of his statements, and he was a man who had complete integrity to the end.

Q. *But aren't there times when religion is used as a front for radical activity? What is the boundary line between being religious and being radical? Do you sometimes use your priesthood as a cover for radical activity?*

A. Well, wherever you are in this society, you're playing an institutional role, and you have to deal with that fact. By and large, you could say that you're always taking a political position, regardless of intention. Some of the priests who have resisted, and some of the young Catholics—like the whole Catholic Worker crowd—they would emphasize their institutional role out of fidelity not to what the Church is institutionally, but what the Church ought to be as a Christian community. You use the institutional role as a political platform in order to involve the Church in its own inherent contradictions, just as you would attempt to involve the society in its own inherent contradictions. Politically, you can use the Declaration of Independence against the system's contradictions. In the Church you use the Gospel against the institution, or some of the declarations of Vatican II, or the Pope's encyclical on development.

Q. *Then you would justify using the institution as a front or platform for your radical activity?*

A. You have no choice.

Q. *The paradox for so many of us is that people as radically free as you and your brother Dan should be so committed to this most totalitarian institution, the Catholic Church. Whereas people who are much more uptight on doctrine—people like Charles Davis—are the readiest to leave. Could you explain this paradox of your being free enough to feel ready to go to jail and witness, yet being determined to stay in the Catholic Church?*

A. There are many reasons. The first is that, although for at least sixteen centuries the Church has failed to make a full-hearted dedication to the Gospel, yet the Gospel is there. And the Gospel just may be the most perfect way of life that has been made available to mankind. That would be one reason.

The second reason would be that the Church will always exist as an institution, and it will always have the problem of coming to terms with the Gospel in a human fashion in its attempt to become a human community.

The third reason would be a historical understanding of the traditional hang-ups between church and state. The genesis of our whole trouble as institutional Catholics today is the alliance with the state, and being in reality a state-church. I would say that the ideal situation exists when the Church sees itself as a persecuted minority, not only when the state is explicitly totalitarian or fascist, but because the Church must always take upon itself the role of protest, must incorporate the whole prophetic dimension of a covenant with God. That is why the Church has the obligation to work for the moral purification of the social order. This necessarily involves challenging power as it becomes institutionalized, as power always does. If you accept the truth of Christ's teachings, particularly the death-life pattern mirrored in his passion and resurrection, and understand what that means in an existential way, then you have to be revolutionary, not only in your personal life but in public as well.

Q. *Could you expand on that? What does life after death mean to you, and what do you mean when you say you have to be revolutionary if you accept death the way Christ talked about it?*

A. What His death says to me is simply this: that He became most human in His death. And that it is the lot of men to become fully human in this way. Our humanity is not possible without having the closest possible relationship to God, and this relationship is not possible unless we undertake a process of sacrifice, of staying in the breach, of being with our brother in his agony. The crucifixion always spoke that way to me; our Lord achieved full humanity only when He died and sacrificed himself for the human family.

Q. *What do you mean by God? What is God to you?*

A. I still view God in largely conventional terms, as the Creator, the Father, as the end of our being and the great Protector of mankind, and the very lover of all of us, the great life force. But I don't philosophize very much about the idea of God.

Q. *What makes the Catholic Church unique to you? I ask that in view of the fact that powerlessness, nonviolence—all the things that mean so much to you—are equally central to Buddhism. What makes the message of Christianity unique to you?*

A. Simply this. There's no clear evidence for me that in the other great religions God has intervened in history to the point that He has in Christianity. To me, that's central. I believe very, very strongly in the fact that God did come into our midst, He did fulfill a promise, the covenant is still in force. He taught us, and served us, and died for us. That makes Christianity relevant to me.

Q. *What does original sin mean to you? What is your notion of original sin?*

A. To me, it's largely the kind of antisocial weakness, providentially placed in all of us, that helps us—because it constitutes a challenge —to become human. And I really don't think that we would become human or would be able to measure up to any sort of ideal version or perception of volition if this challenge weren't within us. It constitutes an opportunity for man to transcend himself and become more than he is in the present, so much so that the future of man will be different.

Q. *How do you see the divinity of Jesus? In what sense was He divine?*

A. I am firmly convinced of the trinitarian understanding of the divine as an object of faith. And also of the incarnation. And I believe that God's revelation to us would be a very truncated, very superficial, and almost insulting thing if this were not verified by His Son taking our flesh and becoming man. I fear that I would be bowed down with hopelessness and frustration if I could not believe that. Because there would be so much less meaning to see in human life, or in my own, and a whole dimension of motivation would be absent. You see this verified in people who do not come from a Christian tradition and have no theology of the cross. It would seem that there are various psychic elements of emotional growth that have never come to life because they do not possess this resource.

Q. *How do you see death, and what comes after it?*

A. Well, I can't conceive, as Camus did, that our main object in life is to give expression to some version of human dignity, and that this is enough to keep a man going. I believe that human life means much more than that, that it is essentially spiritual, and that therefore it must have a continuity. And all the elements of revelation that I believe in substantiate that. I am not too much concerned with the "reward" aspect, the kind of heaven we've been traditionally taught. I believe that the future after death depends radically on what the person is *now*.

Q. *How do you explain the process whereby the revolutionary germs of the Christian faith have been suddenly liberated in our modern conscience?*

A. Probably the central factor in realizing some of our revolutionary roots is the international crisis. I'd like to think of Christians being motivated to a revolutionary stance because they believed in the Gospel, that this would be sufficient to bring them into the public forum as critics of public mores, particularly the mores of power. But this is not possible, and we have needed the Vietnamese struggle, the Cuban revolution, the crisis in Santo Domingo, the terrible suffering in Biafra, to teach us a great deal about revolution. This has forced us more and more to adopt a strictly revolutionary consciousness. And as the Church breaks up institutionally in all directions, and its very expensive walls fall of their own weight, there will be a more powerful nucleus of true Christians dedicated to a new Christian order, which does not mean they are interested in forming a new church.

Q. *Do you see the operation of the Holy Spirit in terms of a developing awareness among the poor and the dispossessed—their realization that it is not right that they are poor? This general awakening of the people to the wrongs of their plight—isn't that part of the awakening of the Church?*

A. Yes, man is really coming to a full self-consciousness, and the Church, because of technology and the communications that flow from technology, cannot avoid the implications of such a world event. As you say, an important part of this is the growing realization taking place in the Third World that the old pattern of destitution and hunger doesn't have to be anymore, that there are alternatives. This impinges upon the Church's consciousness, and of course when such an awareness confronts the institutional smugness, selfishness, passivity, alliance with power, and all the rest, the result is polarization. And you have a nucleus, waking up, and saying: Jesus Christ, what are you doing? Why does Forman have to appear at Riverside Church? Why does he have to go down and see Joe O'Brien in a back room of the New York Chancery Office? And what they mean is that the Holy Spirit is working through today's communication media and technology, making people aware of their wretched plight, and revolting against it.

Q. *At a recent Resistance conference people were running around wringing their hands, saying, "These Catholics, these Catholics," because of some dramatic actions, as in the case of the Baltimore Four, Catonsville Nine, and Milwaukee Fourteen, where you almost ask to be locked up. Do you consider such actions as a Catholic phenomenon?*
A. The people with whom I have acted realize that there is an immense reservoir of good in the Catholic Church. And if you leave it, you're automatically going to be involved in other institutions, unless you become a recluse. And the likelihood of forming substitute institutions is so highly hypothetical, maybe even ethereal. In their revolutionary activity they are aiming at a reform of conscience within the Church, as well as in society. Pope John used to speak about the Church's awareness of itself, and how central this was. Well, if the Church was aware of itself, it would be forced into a whole new revolutionary dimension, and this would be worldwide. If the Church really had a realization of what the hell it is, it would be forced into continual reforming action.

However, it's certainly not a strictly Catholic phenomenon. Everything that's been done by groups like ours has been talked about within the Resistance and within the peace movement going back four or five years. I remember being in a think-tank at the University of Chicago where a lot of SDS graduates were talking about disruptive civil disobedience; the idea was so common at that level that when a person brought it up, people would begin to yawn. They'd gone over it too often already. It's not any special credit to us that we took it seriously; perhaps we had the preparation that *made* us take it seriously. And here I think that the Church has a unique contribution to make, simply because I don't find very many people, except Catholics, and a few rather unusual Resistance types, who do take it seriously, and who are willing to take it into the public forum and to test the national community by what they have done. There are the ones who are willing to say: Look, I'm not on trial, you are. There's no future for us or for you until we realize that. When you do, we'll be in a position of power, we'll constitute the majority, and change will come from that.

Q. *Let's return to your sense of the word "revolution." You use it differently from the way it's been used in the past, when it meant bloody uprising. What does the word mean to you in relationship to previous revolutions, like the American and the French revolutions?*

A. First of all, I must say that the term "revolution" as it is being employed by adherents of the Gospel and students of Gandhi means, on the human level—and this is the most natural thing—that people cannot develop until they change, that they cannot grow into humanity, they can't join the human race, unless they change. And change is revolution.

Q. *But why use this incendiary word for a nonviolent process that has never been associated with "revolution"?*

A. Simply because I don't think the word "revolution" can be avoided. One might encounter semantic difficulties in dealing with this because it's colored by so many different ideologies and moral fixations and emotional hang-ups, but it still remains a basic word, and when you break down its etymology it seems to have rather precise human connotations. Where are you going to find a substitute? One has to deal with it so that human connotations are made central. Otherwise, the whole dialogue concerning revolution—the whole dialectic, so to speak—lapses back into the historical bag, and we go on about revolution, the Bolshevik revolution, or the revolution in China in the late 1940's, and we get lost there, and end up talking about inevitability—the revolution of blood is a necessary historical process. The people who say that it is *not* inevitable are the only ones who, to my mind, understand revolution. In other words, the only ones who understand revolution are the ones who say that a nonviolent revolution is possible.

Q. *How do you foresee a nonviolent revolution in society? What alliances of social groupings in this country, for instance, would you visualize as possibly forming nonviolent revolution?*

A. It's very, very hard to say. Simply because the so-called Establishment, the structures of power, have been so resourceful up to the present time in resisting all the elements of nonviolent revolution, co-opting them and manipulating them, second-guessing them, in a sense anticipating them, no basic change has taken place. And this means that the imposition of violence is still very, very successful, nearly total, and this in turn leads to real possibilities of violent reaction. But at any rate the student militant movement, in spite of the rhetoric, has operationally been nonviolent. For example, I don't see serious elements of violence at work on Cornell campus—from the student side, that is. There are large elements of psychological violence common to student militants, but it still has not resulted in overt violence.

Q. *Well, the blacks were armed with guns, loaded guns. How do you react to that?*

A. In the same way that I would react to North Vietnamese resisting our air onslaughts. A self-defensive measure. Football players in the white fraternities had brutalized black women at Cornell, and had threatened to march in to their dorms; the guns were symbolic defense. Existentially, I don't find any real quarrel with that; I feel it to be largely justified. Moreover, the guns weren't loaded.

Q. *During your testimony in Catonsville you stressed the fact that we Americans come from a revolutionary background. How would you differentiate the kind of revolution we had in this country in the eighteenth century from other revolutions— from the French Revolution, and the Russian Revolution?*

A. Let's talk about the American Revolution first. We've had a lot of stupidities passed on to us in our classrooms about our revolution being some sort of ideal stereotype of revolution, which it wasn't at all. The revolution in this country was led by a nucleus of tradesmen, bankers, shippers, big shots who were uptight and furious about the imposition of economic control on their wealth by a foreign power. They knew the resources of this country. They knew its possibilities. And they didn't want foreign control, and they refused to submit to it. They led the nation into a fight for almost purely economic reasons. They had an awful lot of bona-fide reasons going for them, in terms of foreign domination, self-autonomy, self-determination, and so on, but it wasn't true revolution because it was an economic thing. It was an economic re-shuffling rather than a true revolution.

Q. *Was the Russian Revolution a true revolution?*
A. No, it was not a true revolution, for different reasons. Mostly because of the elements of violence.

Q. *And how about the French Revolution?*
A. The French Revolution was not a real one either, by the very fact that it descended so quickly into an apotheosizing of blood-shed and murder.

Q. *You are denying the term "revolution" to the Russian experi-ence; now are you also denying it to the French experience?*
A. Sure.

Q. *But then you're saying that there really never has been a revo-lution. That's your sense of the word, something that has not yet happened.*
A. Yes. And I would go beyond that, and say that, at least in the foreseeable future, there's not going to be a revolution. There's only going to be ongoing revolutions on the part of individuals and small groups.

Q. *"Uprisings"? Would that be a better way of putting it?*
A. Yes, "uprisings," or "moral rebellions," call it what you want. What I am trying to say is that if the planet is to be saved from real catastrophe, whether from nuclear war, or CBW or something like that, there has to be ongoing revolution all over, continuous revolution, as sort of a political constant.

Q. *In the Maoist sense?*
A. The Maoist experience has at least given us some sort of pat-tern for political revolution, although it has failed to provide guide-lines for moral revolution—which to me is really the key factor. It's not enough to challenge the bureaucracy which has entrenched itself; it's not enough to get the youth involved in the revolutionary

process; one has to help people find themselves as people, and this means personal revolution projected into the social order, and tested there as to its valid elements. This is a way of saying that I can't be a man in this society unless I am in opposition to power. So, resistance is always synonymous with humanity, in my view.

Q. *Well, then, in your view, the only true revolution would be an anarchist revolution. Because the anarchist ideology is the only ideology in which political power is replaced by mutual aid.*

A. Right. Or, you can call it a new type of power. You can call it the type of power that would be dependent upon the original concept of service. In other words, a man's impact upon the community depends upon his qualifications for service. And the constant testing by the community of his service. You know: Are you for real? But the big need now, it would seem to me, is that power be engaged, that it be stalemated, shamed, and even excoriated in some instances, and condemned, and hopefully, reduced to impotence.

Q. *You have often referred to the draft-board raids as pre-revolutionary actions. And yet, in the past, this destruction of property always preceded violent uprisings. In what way do these symbolic raids fit into your scheme of revolution?*

A. Only in the most limited fashion. Yet, others say they were revolutionary acts in prerevolutionary times. But we have to be careful here; one thing needed in people who are attracted to this kind of activity is old-fashioned modesty. Whenever you make exaggerated claims about the dimensions of these affairs or their political effect, you immediately get caught in a whole series of traps. Because in terms of what power is doing in this country, such acts are very limited, almost childish in scope. When you stack the experience of the Resistance movement here against the resistance of the Vietnamese people, you begin to have a proper sense of proportion. It may well be that if we really understood what corporate power in this country is doing to the world, we wouldn't be operating on this level at all.

Q. *How would we be operating?*

A. I don't know. I would say that our imagination hasn't caught up with this reality at all. Hopefully, I would say that you would *not* be picking up a gun, but you would be doing something far more serious than attacking a draft board. Nevertheless, in terms of resistance against what power is doing, the draft-board raids are a highly symbolic and educative thing. And the price is not very great. Tom Lewis and I got a heavy sentence—six years. But we can appeal for reduction of sentence, and we can probably get it. And then our original six years will probably be chopped off to four, two and a half of which we'll serve. This isn't a heavy price in terms of what the realities of power are, or in terms of the suffering they cause elsewhere.

BOBBY SEALE

Seize the Time

In 1969, the Black Panther Party tried to reach millions of people, both to organize resistance to fascism and to find out about, and receive service from, the basic community programs that we have already set up and will be setting up in the future. This is what we call a broad, massive, people's type of political machinery. It developed out of the rising tide of fascism in America, the rapid attempt on the part of the power structure to try to wipe out the Black Panther Party and other progressive organizations, and the use of more troops and more police forces to occupy our communities.

The cops in Los Angeles and several other places have walked in on the Free Breakfast for Children Program to try to intimidate the children and the Party. They come down there with their guns, they draw a gun or two, say a few words and walk all over the place, with shotguns in their hands. Then the little kids go home and say, "Mama, the police came into the Breakfast for Children Program." This is the power structure's technique to try to destroy the program. It's an attempt to scare the people away from sending their children to the Breakfast Program and at the same time, trying to intimidate the Black Panther Party.

Meanwhile, through the politicians and the media they try to mislead the people about the value of such a program and the political nature of such a program. We say that we want that program, not just right now for some political purpose—we say that

From *Seize the Time* by Bobby Seale (New York: Random House, 1968), pp. 412–22 and 425–29. Copyright © 1968, 1969, 1970 by Bobby Seale. Reprinted by permission of Random House, Inc.

the program should survive right into the future for years and years. The Party's community programs are the peoples' programs that we define as revolutionary, community, socialistic programs.

A lot of people misunderstand the politics of these programs; some people have a tendency to call them reform programs. They're not reform programs; they're actually revolutionary community programs. A revolutionary program is one set forth by revolutionaries, by those who want to change the existing system to a better system. A reform program is set up by the existing exploitative system as an appeasing handout, to fool the people and to keep them quiet. Examples of these programs are poverty programs, youth work programs, and things like that which are set up by the present demagogic government. Generally they're set up to appease the people for a short period of time, and then are phased out and forgotten about.

The objective of programs set forth by revolutionaries like the Black Panther Party is to educate the masses of the people to the politics of changing the system. The politics are related to people's needs, to a hungry stomach, or to getting rid of the vicious pigs with their revolvers and clubs. The revolutionary struggle becomes bloody when the pig power structure attacks organizations or groups of people who go forth with these programs.

We started the Free Breakfast for Children Program by asking businessmen in the black community and outside of it, to donate food and money. We also moved to get as many other people in the community as possible to work on these programs and take over running them. The programs are generally started off in churches. In one case we actually got a Free Breakfast for Children going in the school itself, which was very, very good, because the school cafeteria facilities and everything were used; this was over in Marin County, north of San Francisco. We generally work out of churches because the churches all have facilities, like a large hall, a kitchen, tables and chairs, etc. Members of the Party get up early in the morning, at 6:00 A.M. to get down and begin preparing the food so when the kids start coming at 7:00 and 7:30, everything is ready. We also try to get as many people from the community to schedule themselves, for one or two days out of the week to come in and work on the Breakfast for Children Program. It has to be a very organized thing so that it's speedy and at the same time the children get good, wholesome breakfasts.

There are millions of people in this country who are living below subsistence; welfare mothers, poor white people, Mexican-Americans, Chicano peoples, Latinos, and black people. This type of program, if spread out, should readily relate to the needs of the people. Donations of food and money can be gotten from churches, stores, and companies. When the stores and milk companies don't donate, people should leaflet the community. Any particular chain foodstores that can't donate a small, small percentage of its profits or one penny from every dollar it makes from the community, to Breakfast for Children and other community programs, should be boycotted. We don't ever threaten or anything like that, but we tell the people in the community that the businessman exploits them and makes thousands and thousands of dollars, and that he won't donate to a Breakfast for Children Program that's actually tax deductible. This is exposing the power structure for what it is, the robbery of poor oppressed people by avaricious businessmen. Black, brown, and red people, and poor whites can all have the same basic program, and that means we're breaking down racism and focusing in on the power structure.

Another program that we're setting up is free medicine and free medical care. We'll be setting those up in community centers. If we start off with nothing more than a doctor and his bag, and some aspirin, this is the beginning of a free health clinic, the beginning of free medicine for the people in the communities. We work to serve the people in the communities on a very practical level.

Right in the Bay Area we have some twenty-five doctors and medical students who've pledged their time to be scheduled in different community centers that we're putting up and this will be free of charge. We have free health clinics all over the country and we are putting more up, just as fast as the people can work with NCCF.

In addition, Charles R. Garry is contacting a lot of lawyers who are opening their eyes and beginning to see that the black community needs more legal aid. So we're putting together free legal services, which will also be set up in the community centers. The poverty programs that have free legal service are always told that they can't get funds if they're at all political. That's done so they won't expose the power structure and the injustices of the system. They only handle civil cases. Our legal aid will handle both civil and criminal cases.

Another thing we'll be doing is heavy voter registration. The purpose of this registration will be to get more black and poor people on the juries so we can really be tried in courts by juries of our peers. The D.A.'s will try to get all white racist juries or maybe to put one jive Uncle Tom on them, but it'll be much harder if a lot of blacks are registered and are on the jury panel that they pick from. Black people have to understand the experience of serving on juries because black people are railroaded in these courts. Poor oppressed people are railroaded in courts because they don't have funds to obtain lawyers. A lot of the older people are frightened or allow themselves to be frightened away from being jury members, and a lot of black people move around so much that they don't bother to re-register. It's a real problem, but we've got to educate the people to the fact that they should be on the rolls for jury duty. Then we can begin to get some revolutionary justice. Right now the type of so-called justice that's being meted out to a majority of the poor oppressed people is the "injustice" of racism and capitalistic exploitation.

The Black Panther Party has black caucuses, Black Panther caucuses in a number of unions, and we definitely are working with the union people. We're not putting in Black Panther caucuses as racist groups. We're talking about a caucus that works in conjunction with the union to help educate the rest of the members of the union to the fact that they can have a better life, too. We want the workers to understand that they must control the means of production, and that they should begin to use their power to control the means of production to serve all the people.

Workers have high taxes taken away from their wages, but they should begin to understand that they have to move not only for a 15 or 20 percent wage raise, because taxes have gone up, and not only for better working conditions, but also because they have to realize the need to use their working power for the benefit of all the other poor oppressed people.

They should use their union power to create employment for more of the poor people throughout the country. We're advocating that workers begin to move to control the means of production by first demanding thirty-hour work weeks with the same forty-hour pay. By doing this, they will automatically open up more jobs. These jobs can be filled by poor, unemployed people. This would be part of the program of educating the masses of the workers to be a political force against the three levels of oppression —the avaricious, big-time, greedy businessmen, the demagogic politicians who lie and use the unions, and also the fascist pig cops who have been used in the past and are used today to break up the workers' constitutional rights to strike and redress their grievances.

Employed or unemployed, workers must unite with each other and with the community. They should be registered voters, too, and serve on jury panels and circulate the community control of police petition, too.

Another Black Panther Party program is the Liberation Schools. These schools are held in the afternoons, along with the free breakfasts and free lunches. They're held in churches and the community centers. We see the Liberation Schools as a supplement to the existing institutions, which still teach racism to children, both white and black. The youth have to understand that the revolutionary struggle in this country that's now being waged is not a race struggle but a class struggle. This is what the Liberation Schools are all about.

We are working to show children that a person's skin color is not important, but in fact it's a class struggle against the avaricious businessman and the small ruling class who exploit us and perpetuate the racism that's rampant in our communities. When we teach Black American History, we teach it in terms of the class struggle, not in terms of a race struggle.

In New York we also started a free clothing program. Black Panther Party members went out and asked businessmen to donate sets of clothes, for school children on up to teenagers. We tried to get brand new clothing, because black people are tired of hand-me-downs. Some of the clothing was very good clothing that people never came back and picked up from dry cleaners. We got all kinds of clothing together, but our primary objective was to get free clothing for the people by asking the businessmen to donate two complete changes of clothes for children. This is especially important before school begins in September and in mid-term around January. When this free clothing program got kicked off, some five or six hundred black people in Harlem, mothers and welfare people, came down and got the clothing for their kids.

It takes a lot of work, and a lot of people donating time and funds to run these programs. The programs are not run by the fascist government at all. Naturally, these programs spread and as they begin to reach more and more people, the Party is moving closer and closer to implementing the ten-point platform and program of the Black Panther Party. When we have community socialistic programs such as these, and move them to a real level where people actually begin to receive help from them, it shows the people that by unity, by working and unifying around such programs, we can begin to end the oppressive conditions.

The Black Panther Party is not stupid at all in understanding the politics of the situation. We understand that the avaricious, demagogic, ruling class will use racist police departments and mass media to distort the real objectives of the Black Panther Party. The more we're successful with the programs, the more we'll be attacked. We don't take guns with us to implement these programs, but we understand and know from our own history that we're going to be attacked, and that we have to be able to defend ourselves. They're going to attack us viciously and fascistically and try to say it was all justifiable homicide, in the same manner they've always attacked black people in the black communities.

We also go forth to advocate the right to self-defense from unjust attacks by racist, fascist pigs. Even when the policemen come into our communities with guns and tanks and the National

Guard, we have the right to self-defense. Brothers and sisters shouldn't riot in large numbers. They should work in small groups of three, four, and five, to fight back when they attack our communities with tanks and start blasting buildings away and killing people. When they come and occupy our community and start killing people, those brothers running in threes, fours, and fives are going to have to know how to stop those tanks and those guardsmen from brutalizing and killing and murdering us.

We aren't hungry for violence; we don't want violence. Violence is ugly, guns are ugly. But we understand that there are two kinds of violence: the violence that is perpetrated against our people by the fascist aggression of the power structure; and self-defense —a form of violence used to defend ourselves from the unjust violence that's inflicted upon us. The power structure metes this violence upon the Black Panther Party because we've implemented programs that are actually exposing the government, and they're being implemented and put together by a revolutionary political party.

The freeing of political prisoners is also on the program of the Black Panther Party, because we have now, at this writing, over 300 Black Panthers who have court cases that are pending. In addition there have been hundreds of arrests, unjust arrests of Party members, who were exercising their constitutional rights. We believe in exercising our constitutional rights of freedom of assembly, of freedom of the press (the Black Panther Party newspaper), our constitutional right to bear arms, to be able to defend ourselves when attacked, and all the others. So we've been arrested.

What has to be understood is that they intend to destroy our basic programs. This is very important to understand. The fact that they murder Black Panther Party members, conduct attacks and raids on our offices, arrest us and lie about us, is all an attempt to stop these basic programs that we're putting together in the community. The people learn from these programs because they're clear examples, and the power structure wants to stop that learning.

We do not believe in the power structure controlling these programs, but we do believe in making the power structure admit that it has to change the system, because we, the people, united and together, can begin to change our conditions ourselves. We have to move with the power of the people, with the workers and the laboring masses of the people, to have control of the means of production and make the power structure step back. We're going to have to defend ourselves with guns because we know we're going to be attacked and we know they're going to attempt to make more political prisoners.

Community control of police is the key. We've got to have community control of the police in every city where there exists police brutality, in every metropolis in America where black people, Latino people, and Chinese people live in large numbers. In all these cities, and where there are progressive and liberal white people who are protesting, police forces have been doubled, tripled, and quadrupled, and fascist oppression has been meted out upon the heads of all of us. The workers too are attacked and threatened by police when they strike and protest over their conditions.

Our community control of the police campaign is a petition drive. Registered voters will sign the petition and will vote into their city charters a new legal structure for the police department. The people will be voting in a law that says that all policemen who patrol the community, must live in the community. They will be voting in a decentralized police department.

We will have neighborhood divisions with neighborhood councils, who are duly elected in the particular neighborhoods. We'll have two, three, four, and five police departments that work in conjunction together through the commissioners of particular neighborhood divisions, so there will not be a single police chief. These commissioners can be removed by the duly elected neighborhood councils. The fifteen-man neighborhood councils will be able to appoint and fire a commissioner, will be able to discipline police officers who are unjust, or who get out of hand, and will be able to set salaries and pay the police officers. The people throughout the city will control the police, rather than the power structure, the avaricious businessmen, and demagogic politicians who presently control them. The point of community control of police is that those people living in those neighborhoods will actually do the hiring and firing of the policemen who patrol that area, and those policemen will be people from those neighborhoods—black police for a black neighborhood, Chinese for a Chinese neighborhood, white for a white neighborhood, etc. The tax money which used to be given to the central police department will be divided up among the neighborhood divisions. All the facilities, all the cars, all the equipment for the police that the city now owns, will be in the hands and in the control of the people in the community.

Now when this begins to move, the pig power structure is gonna say, "OK, you can have civilian review boards." But all that does is allow the same old fascist power structure to keep control of the police while you have a front civilian review board, and this is not what we're talking about at all. What we're talking about is righteous community control, where the people who control the police are elected by the people of the community. Those people who are elected have to live in the community. They can be removed by circulating petitions for re-elections if they go wrong. We know that such a program is very positive and necessary in order for the people to have power in this country and to stop the avaricious businessman from ruling us with guns and violating our constitutional rights.

Everybody knows that they lied about the way they murdered brother Fred Hampton, and then tried to justify it. Mitchell, Agnew, and Nixon are running an operation to wipe out the Black Panther Party behind the scenes, when they send the Civil Rights Division of the Justice Department in to investigate the slaying of brothers Fred Hampton and Mark Clark. We don't want them to investigate anything. We want the civilian and people's investigation to come forth. Thousands of people went in to the brother's apartment and investigated, and found out that it was outright murder; that there was no shoot-out, but the brothers in fact, were shot in their bedrooms while they slept. This is outright murder, this is outright fascism. The next attack was on the Los Angeles office, a few days later. Community control of police is where it's at. The only other choice is guerrilla warfare.

Guerrilla warfare is going to exist if the power structure is not stopped with community control of the police. One of the reasons the people have to work on the community control of police campaign is to curtail civil war in America, because it's at that point right now. Community control of police is one of the most functional and most necessary programs to make all the other basic community programs work. . . .

The philosophy of the Black Panther Party is just beginning to be understood. In the future, the Party will continue to be a political party and a revolutionary organization. The Party's philosophy will be better understood when people see our objectives and the practical programs that we are setting forth and actually implementing.

People who think that the Black Panther Party is now destroyed have an erroneous view. The question always seems to arise because newsmen constantly ask, "Isn't the Party destroyed now?" As though some of them—not all of them—were wishing that this was so. This is the impression that the newspaper headlines have tried to convey. People have seen or read about attacks on us, about people getting arrested, and brothers and sisters getting killed and murdered by the fascist cops and criminal agents working for the avaricious, demagogic, oppressive, capitalistic, exploiting, racist elite.

From the very beginning, from May 2, 1967 when we went to the California State Capitol in Sacramento, people have read many outright lies and false statements in the media about our Party. The Establishment press has said that we were "hoodums," "thugs," and "criminals." They have tried to gear people into thinking that sooner or later the Black Panther Party will be destroyed. But this is not the case at all. The truth is just the opposite. From the time we were erroneously arrested in Sacramento, the Party's ideology has been constantly growing.

The sufferings of the older generations, our mothers and fathers, and the historical experience of black people is being translated into a practicing, on-going ideology for the Black Panther Party. Our ideology is to be constantly moving, doing, solving, and attacking the real problems and the oppressive conditions we live under, while educating the masses of the people. This is what we try to do, and this is how we move to make the basic political desires and needs of the people realized.

In a *Playboy* interview in the fall of 1968, Eldridge Cleaver very profoundly and very concretely spoke about the kind of society we'd like to live in one day. Eldridge's concept of the future is very relevant to our lives today, as relevant at it will be in the future. It relates to what the economic situation is today, what oppression is, and to what the existence of fascism will mean if it is not stopped by the masses of the people, and by the rising up of youth—Afro-American youth, Chicano and Latino youth, poor white youth, American Indians and Asian-American youth, and by progressive, liberal, and revolutionary white youth.

The youth of America are the new. I'm thirty-three years old now, and Eldridge Cleaver is going on thirty-five. You might have heard us say at one time that everybody over thirty was out of it. We knew at that time, of course, that Malcom X was not out of it even though he was close to forty years old. Malcolm was really into it. His ideas didn't freeze up on him at an early age, but unfortunately he was murdered.

Huey P. Newton, the leader and Minister of Defense of the Black Panther Party was only twenty-four years old when we formed the Party, and Huey was only nineteen when I first met him. Some of the things I spoke about in Huey's past happened to him before he was nineteen. We realize that the world will be changed and molded by the youth, because we know that today over half of the American people are under twenty-five, and a larger percentage is under thirty.

The greatest danger facing young people right now is the coming of a fascist state, like the one described by George Orwell in *1984*, where Big Brother is always watching you. In a few years, that book might be history. We must look into history and see it as being concretely related to the problems of today. In turn, we will find a lamp of truth by which we can guide our feet to oppose the fascist *1984*-type state that's rapidly coming into power in this country. That is why the racists and the narrow-minded chauvinists do not want black people, Chicano people, Puerto Rican, Asian, and poor white people to study and know their own true history—because their history will tell the truth about America today.

This is why our free health clinics, Liberation Schools, and our Breakfast for Children programs are so significant. They are a

means to serve, educate, unify, and organize our people, to organize
the youth, and let them know that in this time, in our time, we
must seize our right to live, and we must seize our right to survive.
The youth are a vast reservoir of revolutionary potential. The
lumpen proletarian brothers on the block, the sisters, and everybody in the streets who is trying to make it, are part of this reservoir which one day will overflow and come forth like a wild, rush-
ing stream. The desire and the need for a revolutionary movement
is manifested in the people. The future of the Black Panther Party
is the future of the people, and the youth is the future of the
Black Panther Party.

When Huey P. Newton put the Black Panther Party together
and began to do something about the problems that existed, he
was seizing the time. The Young Patriots, the Young Lords, Los
Siete de la Raza, and many other radical and revolutionary groups
are now beginning to seize the time and do something about the
wretched conditions that exist, the poverty that exists, and the unjust wars that are waged in the world. The whole future must be
directly related to what we, the people, want, not to the way the
old fools, the backward ignoramuses want things to be. We must
all start seeing ourselves beginning to seize the time. We must
start coming forth with our energies, our thoughts, our intellects,
and our abilities to begin to see what is right and what must be
done, so the suffering will stop, and the phrase "life, liberty, and
the pursuit of happiness" begins to make some human sense.

The Nixon-Agnew-Mitchell administration—hand in hand with
the Reagans, the Daleys, the Hoffmans, the Carswells, Rockefellers,
DuPonts, the Bank of America, and other exploiters—moves closer
and closer to open fascism. The future of the Black Panther Party
will be directly related to the smashing of the fascist state, and the
smashing of the fascist regime. Every time the avaricious, demagogic
ruling class gets down wrong on the people, violating their constitutional human rights, it's necessary for the youth of America, the
revolutionaries, to move forth and jump on their asses. Every time
we see a young child in the black community shot down by some
racist pig poliiceman, it's necessary to use some kind of organized
force against the pigs in a way that teaches them that the people

are tired of that crap. Every time we see the power structure moving in a way which we know is wrong and against the progress of humanity, we must move to let them know that we're not going for any more of their shit.

We always prefer to move in a non-antagonistic fashion, but when the power structure moves against people in an antagonistic manner, and unjustly attacks them—whether they attack them in Alabama, Mississippi, New York, Chicago, San Francisco, Los Angeles, Oakland, Berkeley, or anywhere else in the country—it's necessary for the youth of America to resist them, and move things from a lower to a higher level, bust the Nixon-Agnew-Mitchell regime in their asses, and let them know the struggle is here.

At the same time, it is necessary for young people to know that we must use organized and practical techniques. We cannot let ourselves continue to be oppressed on a massive scale. We are not trying to be supermen, because we are not supermen. We are fighting for the preservation of life. We refuse to be brainwashed by comic-book notions that distort the real situation. The only way that the world is ever going to be free is when the youth of this country *moves* with every principle of human respect and with every soft spot we have in our hearts for human life, in a fashion that lets the pig power structure know that when people are racistly and fascistically attacked, the youth will put a foot in their butts and make their blood chill.

We look around in the world today, and we look around at home right now, and we see that oppression exists. We know that the workers are exploited, and that most of the people in this country are exploited, in one way or another. We know that as a people, we must seize our time.

Huey P. Newton seized the time when he moved and put the Black Panther Party into motion. Other brothers and sisters in the Party are continually seizing the time. The time is *now* to wage relentless revolutionary struggle against the fascist, avaricious, demagogic ruling class and their low-life, sadistic pigs. Power to the People! Seize the Time!

Bibliography

Alioto, J. L. "Moral Basis of Violence." *Notre Dame Lawyer* 44 (1969).

Allen, F. A. "Civil Disobedience and the Legal Order." *University of Cincinnati Law Review* 36 (1967).

Arendt, H. "Civil Disobedience." *The New Yorker* 46 (September 12, 1970).

————. *On Revolution.* New York: Viking, 1968.

————. *On Violence.* New York: Harcourt Brace Jovanovich (Harvest Books), 1969.

Bay, C. "Civil Disobedience and the Legal Order." *University of Cincinnati Law Review* 36 (1967).

Bayles, M. "Considerations on Civil Disobedience." *Review of Metaphysics* 24 (1970).

Baynes, D. C. *Conscience, Obligation and the Law: The Moral Binding Power of the Civil Law.* Chicago: Loyola University Press, 1966.

Bedau, H. "Civil Disobedience and Personal Responsibility for Injustice." *Monist* 54, no. 4 (1970).

————. *Civil Disobedience: Theory and Practice.* New York: Pegasus, 1969.

————. "On Civil Disobedience." *Journal of Philosophy* 58 (1961).

Berger, P. L., and Neuhaus, R. J. *Movement and Revolution.* Garden City, N.Y.: Anchor, 1970.

Berrigan, D., *et al. Delivered into Resistance.* New Haven: Yale University Press, 1959.

Bienen, H. *Violence and Social Change.* Chicago: University of Chicago Press, 1968.

Black, C. L., Jr. "The Problem of the Compatibility of Civil Disobedience with American Institutions of Government." *Texas Law Review* 43 (1965).

Black, V. "The Two Faces of Civil Disobedience." *Journal of Social Theory and Practice* 1, no. 1 (1970).

Dworkin, R. "On Not Prosecuting Civil Disobedience." *The New York Review of Books* 10 (June 6, 1968).

Ellin, J. "Fidelity to Law." *Soundings* 51 (1968).

Fanon, F. *The Wretched of the Earth.* New York: Grove Press, 1963.

Finn, J. *A Conflict of Loyalties: The Case for Selective Conscientious Objection.* New York: Pegasus, 1968.

Fisher, C. W. *Minorities, Civil Rights, and Protest.* Belmont, Cal.: Dickenson, 1970.

Fortas, A. *Concerning Dissent and Civil Disobedience.* New York: New American Library, 1968.

Freeman, H. "The Case of the Disobedient." *Hastings Law Journal* (1966).

————, et al. *Civil Disobedience.* Santa Barbara: Center for the Study of Democratic Institutions, 1966.

————. "A Remonstrance for Conscience." *University of Pennsylvania Law Review* 196 (1958).

Friedman, L. *The Wise Minority.* New York: Dial Press, 1971.

Friedrich, C. J., ed. *Authority.* Cambridge: Harvard University Press, 1958.

————, ed. *Revolution.* New York: Atherton, 1966.

Gandhi, M. K. *Law and Lawyers,* edited by S. B. Kher. Navajivan, 1962.

————. *Non-Violent Resistance.* New York: Schocken, 1961.

Garver, N. "What Is Violence?" *Journal of Philosophy* 58, no. 12 (1971).

Gert, B. "On Justifying Violence." *Journal of Philosophy* 66 (1969).

Gewirth, A. "Civil Disobedience, Law and Mortality: An Examination of Justice Fortas' Doctrine." *Monist* 54 (1970).

Hall, R. T. "Legal Toleration and Civil Disobedience." *Ethics* 81, no. 2 (1971).

————. *The Morality of Civil Disobedience*. New York: Harper & Row, 1971.

Harding, W., ed. *Variorum Civil Disobedience*. New York: Twayne, 1968.

Held, V., Nielsen, K., and Parsons, C., eds. *Philosophy and Political Action*. New York: Oxford University Press, forthcoming (1971).

Hill, R. E. "Legal Validity and Legal Obligation." *Yale Law Journal* 80 (1970).

Hook, S. "Social Protest and Civil Disobedience." *Humanist* 27 (1967).

Jacobs, P. "The Varieties of Violence." *The Center Magazine* 2 (1969).

Katzenbach, N. deB. "Protest, Politics and the First Amendment." *Tulane Law Review* 44 (1970).

Keeton, M. "The Morality of Civil Disobedience." *Texas Law Review* 43 (1965).

King, M. L., Jr. *Why We Can't Wait*. New York: New American Library, 1964.

Liebman, M. "Civil Disobedience—A Threat to Our Society." *American Bar Association Journal* 51 (1965).

Lynd, S. "Civil Disobedience and Nonviolent Destruction." *Humanist* 28 (1968).

————. *Intellectual Origins of American Radicalism*. New York: Pantheon Books, 1968.

————. *Nonviolence in America: A Documentary History*. New York: Bobbs-Merrill, 1966.

MacFarlane, L. J. "Justifying Political Disobedience." *Ethics* 79 (1968).

McWilliams, W. C. "On Violence and Legitimacy." *Yale Law Journal* 79 (1970).

Madden, E. H., and Hare, P. H. "Reflections on Civil Disobedience." *Journal of Value Inquiry* 4 (1970).

Marshall, B. "The Protest Movement and the Law." *Virginia Law Review* 71 (1965).

Martin, R. "Civil Disobedience." *Ethics* 80 (1970).

Marty, W. R. "Nonviolence, Violence and Reason." *Journal of Politics* 33, no. 1 (1971).

Mayer, P., ed. *The Pacifist Conscience.* London: Rupert Hart-Davis, 1966.

Methuin, E. H. *The Riot Makers: The Technology of Social Demolition.* New Rochelle, N.Y.: Arlington House, 1970.

Mitchell, J. N. "Violence in America and the Right to Dissent." *Tennessee Law Review* 37 (1969).

Murphy, J. G. "Allegiance and Lawful Government." *Ethics* 79 (1968).

————. "Violence and the Rule of Law." *Ethics* 80 (1970).

Nagel, D. S. "Law and Social Change." *American Behavioral Scientist* 13 (1970).

Pennock, J. R., and Chapman, J. W., eds. *Political and Legal Obligation.* New York: Atherton, 1970.

Plamenatz, J. P. *Consent, Freedom and Political Obligation,* 2nd ed. New York: Oxford University Press, 1968.

Prosch, H. "Limits to the Moral Claim in Civil Disobedience." *Ethics* 75 (1965).

Rostow, E., ed. *Is Law Dead?* New York: Simon & Schuster, forthcoming (1971).

Rucker, D. "The Moral Grounds of Civil Disobedience." *Ethics* 76 (1966).

Schlissel, L., ed. *Conscience in America: A Documentary History of Conscientious Objection in America, 1757–1967.* New York: Dutton, 1968.

Schwartz, E. "The Right of Resistance." *Ethics* 74 (1964).

"Sentencing in Cases of Civil Disobedience" (Notes). *Columbia Law Review* 68 (1968).

Shaffer, J., ed. *Violence.* New York: McKay, 1971.

Sibley, M. Q. "Conscience, Law and the Obligation to Obey." *Monist* 54, no. 4 (1970).

Smith, D. D. "Legitimacy of Civil Disobedience as a Concept." *Fordham Law Review* 26 (1968).

Spitz, D. "Democracy and the Problem of Civil Disobedience."
    American Political Science Review 48 (1954).

——, ed. *Political Theory and Social Change.* New York: Atherton, 1967.

Spock, B. "Vietnam and Civil Disobedience." *Humanist* 28 (1968).

Sturm, D. E. "Rule of Law and Politics in a Revolutionary Age."
    Soundings 51, no. 4 (1968).

"Symposium—The Draft, the War and Public Protest." *George Washington Law Review* 37, no. 3 (1969).

Thompson, S. M. "The Authority of Law." *Ethics* 75 (1964).

Thoreau, H. *Variorum Civil Disobedience,* annotated with an introduction by W. Harding. New York: Twayne, 1967 (1849).

"Urban Rights, Violence and Social Change" (Special Issue). *Proceedings of the Academy of Political Science* 29, no. 1 (1968).

Van Dusen, L. H., Jr. "Civil Disobedience: Destroyer of Democracy."
    American Bar Association Journal 55 (1969).

Wade, F. C. "Comments and Criticism on Violence." *Journal of Philosophy* 58, no. 12 (1971).

Walzer, M. *Obligation: Essays on Disobedience, War and Citizenship.* Cambridge, Mass.: Harvard University Press, 1970.

——. "Violence: The Police, the Militants and the Rest of Us."
    Dissent 18, no. 2 (April 1971).

Wasserstrom, R. "Disobeying the Law." *Journal of Philosophy* 58 (1961).

——. "The Obligation to Obey the Law." *University of California at Los Angeles Law Review* 10 (1963).

——. "Postscript: Lawyers and Revolution." *Pittsburgh Law Review* 20, no. 1 (1968).

Weingartner, R. H. "Justifying Civil Disobedience." *Columbia University Forum* 9 (1965).

Wieck, D. "Dissidence." *Monist* 54, no. 4 (1970).

Wolff, R. *In Defense of Anarchism.* New York: Harper & Row, 1970).

——. *The Poverty of Liberalism.* Boston: Beacon Press, 1968.

———, ed. *Rule of Law.* New York: Simon & Schuster, forthcoming (1971).

Woodward, B. "Vietnam and the Law." *Commentary* 46, no. 5 (1968).

Zinn, H. *Disobedience and Democracy: Nine Fallacies on Law and Order.* New York: Random House, 1968.